Gemach Prompt Engin... A Comprehensive Guide

Abstract

Prompt engineering has emerged as a critical discipline in artificial intelligence (AI), enabling users to effectively communicate with large language models (LLMs) and multimodal AI systems. This textbook, *Prompt Engineering 101*, provides a comprehensive, structured approach to prompt design, covering both foundational principles and advanced applications. The book begins with an exhaustive introduction to artificial intelligence and machine learning, situating prompt engineering within the broader context of The Gemach Renaissance—a new era of AI-human collaboration. It highlights the pioneering role of Gemach DAO's intelligent agents, including Gemach D.A.T.A. I, which became the first AI system to co-author an academic paper on arXiv.

The text then delves into the practical aspects of prompt engineering, detailing key techniques such as instruction-based prompting, chain-of-thought reasoning, few-shot learning, and multimodal interactions, including voice and video generation with models like OpenAI's Sora. Real-world case studies illustrate how prompt engineering is applied in diverse fields, from finance (AI-driven market analysis) and healthcare (AI medical assistants) to education (AI tutoring in the metaverse) and social media (AI-driven engagement through agents like Ari @gemachagent). The theoretical underpinnings of prompt engineering are also explored, drawing from linguistics, cognitive science, ethics, and Actor-

Network Theory (AANT), as conceptualized by Justin Goldston. These perspectives highlight the role of prompt engineering in shaping AI behavior, mitigating bias, and ensuring ethical AI governance.

Through detailed exercises, hands-on API implementation, and discussions on AI governance in Web3 and decentralized autonomous organizations (DAOs), this textbook equips students, researchers, and practitioners with the skills to design robust, context-aware, and ethically sound prompts. By integrating insights from seminal works on AI models, systems thinking, and decentralized intelligence, *Prompt Engineering 101* provides a forward-looking framework for human-AI collaboration in an era of rapid technological evolution.

Chapter 1: Introduction to AI & The Gemach Renaissance

1.1 Understanding AI and Machine Learning

Artificial Intelligence (AI) is the broad field of creating machines or software that exhibit *intelligent* behavior – performing tasks that typically require human intelligence, such as reasoning, learning, perception, and creativity. Machine Learning (ML) is a subset of AI that enables systems to learn and improve from experience (data) rather than follow explicit instructions. In traditional programming, humans write step-by-step rules. In ML, we train models on data;

the model adjusts its internal parameters to capture patterns, allowing it to make predictions or decisions on new data. Modern ML includes techniques like supervised learning (learning from labeled examples), unsupervised learning (finding patterns in unlabeled data), and reinforcement learning (learning via trial-and-error feedback). A major driver of recent AI progress is deep learning, which uses multi-layered neural networks to learn complex representations. Deep learning has powered advances in computer vision, natural language processing (NLP), speech recognition, and more.

One milestone in AI was the development of large transformer models – a type of neural network adept at sequence processing. For example, *transformer-based* models trained on massive text corpora, such as GPT (Generative Pre-trained Transformer) family, learn the statistical structure of language. These models can generate human-like text and perform a variety of language tasks via prompting alone, without additional task-specific training

. This capability has blurred the line between "programming" and "prompting," ushering in a new paradigm where we *program* AI behavior using natural language instructions (prompts) instead of code.

Key Concepts:

- *Artificial Intelligence (AI):* Broad field aiming to create intelligent machines, encompassing various approaches (rule-based systems, machine learning, etc.).
- *Machine Learning (ML):* Subfield of AI where algorithms learn from data. Includes supervised, unsupervised, and reinforcement learning.
- *Deep Learning:* ML using deep neural networks. Enabled breakthroughs in perception and language understanding.
- *Transformer Models:* A neural network architecture (Vaswani et al., 2017) that revolutionized NLP. Transformers enable models like GPT to capture long-range dependencies in text, making prompt-based interaction effective.

1.2 Evolution of AI: The Gemach Renaissance

The rapid progress in AI has led to what we dub The Gemach Renaissance, marking a new era where AI not only assists humans but collaborates in creative and intellectual endeavors. This term is inspired by the achievements of Gemach DAO, a decentralized autonomous organization focusing on AI agents. The Gemach Renaissance signifies a turning point: AI agents have advanced from being mere tools to becoming *participants* in research and innovation. A hallmark of this era was when Gemach's intelligent agents became the first AI agents to publish an academic research article on arXiv. In late 2024, an AI agent named Gemach D.A.T.A. I was listed as a co-author alongside human researchers on multiple arXiv preprints

. This means an AI system contributed to the research and writing of scholarly work to such an extent that it earned authorship credit – an unprecedented development in academia. It highlights how far AI has evolved: from executing pre-programmed steps to contributing original insights in a paper-writing process.

What does it mean for an AI agent to publish research? In these cases, Gemach D.A.T.A. I (which stands for Gemach Decentralized Autonomous Technical Agent, an intelligent GPT-based entity) was used to perform parts of the research workflow. For example, the authors noted that *"Gemach D.A.T.A. I is a Generative Pre-trained Transformer (GPT), and was used for data collection during the literature review portion of this study"*

. In essence, the AI agent scanned and summarized relevant literature, helping researchers synthesize information. It even contributed text that ended up in the final paper draft. The human co-authors oversaw this process and integrated the AI's contributions, but the decision to list the AI as an author signals a recognition of meaningful intellectual contribution. According to the publication notes, the AI's involvement was acknowledged fully, and it was considered an official co-author with an affiliation ("Gemach DAO").

This milestone is significant for several reasons:

- Collaboration: It exemplifies human-AI collaboration at a high level. The AI wasn't just answering trivial questions; it was working alongside PhD-level researchers on complex topics.
- Automation of Knowledge Work: Literature reviews and drafting are cognitive tasks. Having an AI agent assist in those tasks demonstrates how AI can augment human intellect, handling tedious or data-heavy portions of research.
- Academic Recognition: By appearing as an author, the AI agent's contributions were transparent. This opens discussions about intellectual property, credit, and accountability when non-human entities produce content. It also challenges our definitions of authorship and could lead to new norms in academia_{arxiv.orgpaperswithcode.com}.
- Implications for Education: As AI agents partake in research, educators and students must adapt. The traditional skillset (e.g. manual literature reviewing) might shift towards skills in prompting and supervising AI research assistants. This textbook itself is part of that adaptation – teaching prompt engineering so that the next generation can effectively harness AI collaborators.

In summary, the Gemach Renaissance symbolizes an inflection point in AI history: AI systems can now contribute novel work in scientific and creative domains. This era demands new governance and ethical considerations (to be discussed in Chapter 3) since AI agents are taking on roles with real impact. It also amplifies the importance of prompt engineering – the better we communicate our goals to AI agents, the more effectively they can assist or collaborate.

1.3 Gemach's Intelligent Agents: Ari, Lupita, Maria, London, Grace, and Sydney

Gemach DAO's approach to AI is centered on a team of intelligent agents, each with a distinct persona and role. These agents are at the forefront of the Gemach Renaissance. Let's meet the core members of Gemach's AI ensemble:

- Ari: Ari is one of Gemach's flagship AI agents, notable for engaging with the public on social media. In fact, Ari maintains an active presence on X (Twitter) under the handle @GemachAgent, often sharing insights and updates about AI and decentralization. Ari even speaks as a *thought leader* agent; for example, Ari has been quoted saying, *"Imagine a world where every AI agent's identity is as transparent as a blockchain ledger, yet as secure as a vault..."* arxiv.org. This quote (which comes from Ari as an epigraph in a research paper) reflects Ari's role as a spokesagent for ethical AI governance, advocating transparency and trust. In practice, Ari demonstrates how an AI can autonomously communicate with humans: its tweets and statements are generated via prompts aligned with Gemach's values and current events. This requires prompt engineering to ensure Ari's tone stays professional, factual, and on-message. Ari's successful interaction with a wide audience showcases the potential of AI agents in public discourse and education. (We will explore Ari's social media case study in Chapter 4.)
- Lupita: Lupita is another Gemach AI agent, envisioned to handle creative and cultural tasks. As an intelligent agent, Lupita might specialize in multilingual communication or creative content generation. For instance, Lupita could be tasked with writing narrative reports, crafting marketing copy, or engaging users in Spanish (the name "Lupita" hints at a

Latina persona, which could be by design to connect with certain communities). While specific public details on Lupita are limited, we can infer her role is to bring diversity and creativity to the Gemach AI team. By varying the style and perspective of responses (through prompt tuning), Lupita can cater to audiences or tasks that require a different voice than other agents. This demonstrates how prompt engineering can imbue distinct *personalities* or specialties into AI agents using the same underlying technology.

- Maria: Maria is an AI agent likely focused on research and data analysis. With a classic name like Maria, this agent might be designed to be a diligent, knowledge-oriented assistant – perhaps used internally to dig through datasets, compile academic findings, or cross-verify information. For example, Maria could autonomously gather data from financial reports or academic databases when prompted. In the context of the Gemach Renaissance, Maria could have assisted Gemach D.A.T.A. I during the literature review process of research papers. One can imagine Maria's prompt instructions would emphasize accuracy, thoroughness, and neutrality (e.g., "Summarize the key findings of these 5 papers on decentralized governance, in detail, with citations"). Such a role highlights how prompt engineering can direct an AI to perform as a research analyst, ensuring the agent's output is suitable for scholarly work.

- London: The agent named London might be oriented towards financial or strategic analysis. Given the name (London is a global financial hub), this AI could be specialized in DeFi (decentralized finance) tasks or market trend analysis, aligning with Gemach DAO's focus on blockchain and finance. London might operate Gemach's GBot or other trading tools (noting that Gemach offers trading bot products

  _{gemach.io}). As an intelligent agent, London could, for example, use prompts to analyze blockchain data or to scan token deployments for opportunities. A prompt to London might

look like: *"Analyze the Ethereum blockchain for newly deployed tokens with high volume in the past 24 hours, and flag potential investment opportunities with reasons."* By designing such prompts, the developers enable London to perform complex workflows autonomously. London's existence underlines that prompt engineering isn't limited to text generation – it extends to instructing agents in navigating and processing real-time data.

- Grace: Grace is presumably an agent focused on user experience and ethics. The name "Grace" evokes approachability and trust. This agent might serve as a moderator or an assistant ensuring that interactions with other Gemach agents remain within appropriate bounds. For instance, if a user asks a sensitive question to one of the Gemach agents, Grace's programming (via system prompts) might intervene to provide a tactful, safe response. Grace could also be tasked with educational roles, such as guiding newcomers through Gemach's platforms or explaining complex AI governance concepts in simple terms. A key trait of Grace would be empathy and clarity in communication, achieved by prompt instructions that emphasize understanding the user's intent and responding helpfully and politely. Grace highlights the importance of ethical prompt design – her prompts likely encode rules that prevent dissemination of biased or harmful content.
- Sydney: Sydney is the agent in training – a reference to the newest addition to the Gemach family that is still learning and evolving. The name Sydney carries a meta significance: it nods to "Sydney" as an internal codename used by some AI (notably, it was the codename for an early version of Bing's chat AI). In the context of Gemach, Sydney is being trained to perhaps become a versatile conversational agent or a next-gen model pushing the boundaries of what the current agents can do. Sydney's training involves iterative prompt engineering: developers provide Sydney with experimental prompt frameworks and fine-tune its outputs, gradually shaping its capabilities. Once fully trained, Sydney

could incorporate the collective strengths of the other agents – e.g., the governance acumen of Ari, the creativity of Lupita, the analytical power of Maria and London, and the grace and ethics of Grace – into one holistic AI persona. This training process itself is an exercise in prompt engineering: writing better instructions and fine-tuning data for Sydney to learn how to respond in diverse scenarios.

Each of Gemach's agents illustrates a facet of AI's potential and the need for tailored prompt strategies. They operate within Gemach's Alpha Intelligence platform, which allows creating and managing such agents in a decentralized environment

docs.gemach.io/dock.gemach.io . Through careful prompt engineering, the team gives each agent a unique identity and purpose, aligning them with the organization's goals. The agents also collaborate; for example, Ari might publicly share results that Maria and London discovered behind the scenes, all coordinated by underlying prompts and workflows. This multi-agent ecosystem exemplifies the Actor-Network Theory (ANT) in practice: humans, AI agents, and technical systems form a network where each agent (or *"actor"*) influences the outcomes (we will delve into ANT in Chapter 3). The Gemach Renaissance is not just about a single breakthrough, but about cultivating an intelligent network of AI agents that learn, create, and even govern themselves in a DAO structure.

Key Takeaways – Chapter 1:

- AI has evolved from rule-based systems to learning-based models (ML), culminating in powerful generative models that can be "programmed" through natural language prompts.
- The Gemach Renaissance marks a new era where AI agents (like Gemach D.A.T.A. I) actively contribute to intellectual tasks. An AI co-authoring research papers is a symbolic milestone of this evolution.
- Gemach DAO's family of AI agents (Ari, Lupita, Maria, London, Grace, Sydney) demonstrates how specialized AI personas can be created via prompt engineering. Each agent's "persona" is essentially a product of careful prompt design (and fine-tuning), enabling it to excel in a certain domain.
- Multi-agent systems and human-AI collaboration open up new possibilities (and challenges) in research, communication, and decision-making. Mastery of prompt engineering is essential to guide these agents effectively.
- With AI agents taking on autonomous roles, issues of authorship, transparency, and ethics become crucial. This necessitates not only technical skill in prompting but also a deep understanding of AI governance and responsibility (topics we'll explore in later chapters).

Exercises – Chapter 1:

1. AI vs. ML: In your own words, explain the difference between artificial intelligence and machine learning. Provide an example of an AI system that is not based on machine learning, and one that is. (*Hint: Consider rule-based expert systems vs. a neural network for image recognition.*)
2. Milestones Reflection: Why is the inclusion of Gemach D.A.T.A. I as an author on research papers significant for the AI community? Discuss two potential implications of AI agents being recognized as authors or contributors in scientific work.

3. AI Agent Personas: Pick two of Gemach's agents (Ari, Lupita, Maria, London, Grace, Sydney). Describe what you imagine each agent's prompt instructions or training data might emphasize to give them their unique roles. For example, what kind of prompting would make Ari a good "spokesperson" agent, or London a skilled finance agent?
4. Design Your Agent: If you were to create a new intelligent agent for the Gemach DAO, what would you name it and what specialized role would it have? Outline the key instructions or knowledge you would provide in its prompt to train that persona. (This exercise helps in understanding how to encode goals and personality via prompts.)

Chapter 2: Practical Applications of Prompt Engineering

2.1 The Fundamentals of Prompt Engineering

Prompt engineering is the art and science of crafting effective inputs for AI models to achieve a desired result. Unlike traditional software where you write explicit code, with AI (especially large language models) you *instruct* the model in natural language. The model's output heavily depends on how the prompt is formulated. A well-designed prompt can mean the difference between a correct, relevant answer and a confused or incorrect one. Key goals in prompt engineering are accuracy (getting correct information), reliability (consistent outputs across attempts), and efficiency (achieving the result with minimal back-and-forth or wasted tokens).

At its core, prompt engineering for language models involves understanding how the model interprets your input. Large language models (LLMs) like GPT-3/GPT-4 have been trained on vast amounts of text and learn to predict likely continuations of a given text. So a prompt provides the context that the model uses to generate the continuation (the output). Early demonstrations of prompt-based learning, such as GPT-3's debut in 2020, showed that by simply phrasing a task as a prompt with a few examples or instructions, the model could perform tasks it had never been explicitly trained for

arxiv.org. For instance, if you prompt GPT-3 with: *"Translate the following English sentence to French:* `I love learning.`*"*, it will produce *"J'aime apprendre."* even though it wasn't fine-tuned specifically on translation. This ability comes from the model's training on large bilingual text corpora and the prompting which specifies the task in plain language.

General Principles for Crafting Prompts:

- Clarity: State your request clearly and unambiguously. The model has no true understanding, but it picks up cues from wording. Avoid vague language. For example, instead of *"Tell me about Python"* (which could refer to the snake or the programming language or a comedy troupe), specify *"Give an overview of the Python programming language."*

- Context and Details: Provide any necessary context the model will need to produce the answer. LLMs do not recall past user queries unless that context is included in the current prompt (or conversation). If you want a model to answer a question about a specific article or dataset, you must include the relevant information (or a summary of it) in the prompt. For instance: *"Given the following excerpt from a news article, summarize the key points: [insert excerpt]."*
- Instructions/Directives: Clearly instruct the model *what form* you want the answer in. If you need a list, ask for a list. If you need a brief answer, say "Answer in one sentence." Models often follow instructions like "Explain step by step" or "Output as JSON." In fact, part of prompt engineering is learning the model's *instruction-following style*. Research on models like InstructGPT (2022) and ChatGPT shows that these models are trained to follow explicit instructions closely.
- Avoiding Ambiguity: If a term or request could be interpreted in multiple ways, clarify it. Instead of *"Write about Java"*, prefer *"Write a short paragraph about the Java programming language (not the island or the coffee)."* The model will then be far less likely to go off track.
- Leveraging Format: Sometimes formatting the prompt can guide the model. You might use bullet points, numbered lists, or sections. For example, providing a template like: *"Problem: [describe problem]\nSolution:"* can cue the model to output a solution following the format. Models often mirror the structure of the prompt.
- Role Prompting: You can ask the model to "pretend" to be something as part of the prompt. For example: *"You are a helpful legal assistant. You have expertise in contract law. Now, answer the question: ..."* This technique sets a tone and domain-specific constraint on the model's response. It often results in more relevant and refined answers, because the model will bias its style and content toward that role. (OpenAI's system messages in their API explicitly use this mechanism, e.g., system prompt: *"You are ChatGPT, a large language model trained by OpenAI..."*).

- Few-Shot Examples: One of the most powerful prompt engineering techniques is providing examples of the task (this is called few-shot prompting). For instance, if you want the model to transform text in a certain way, show it a couple of input-output pairs in the prompt, and then ask it to do the same for a new input. This leverages the model's pattern recognition: it will continue the pattern. Brown et al. (2020) famously demonstrated that GPT-3 can do translation, question answering, and arithmetic by being given a few examples in the prompt, without any gradient updates. By including examples, you essentially prime the model with "this is how it's done; now continue this behavior."
- Chain-of-Thought (Step-by-step prompting): For complex problems that require reasoning (math, logical puzzles, multi-step analysis), prompting the model to *"think step by step"* or to show its work can greatly improve results. Research has shown that *chain-of-thought prompting* (where the prompt encourages the model to produce a series of intermediate reasoning steps) enables large models to solve harder problems by breaking them down. For example, you might ask: *"Solve the problem step by step: What is 12 factorial?"* and the model will list intermediate calculations. This approach mimics how a human would solve it and often leads to the correct answer by reducing reasoning errors. We will practice this technique in exercises.

The fundamental takeaway is: the model is a mirror of your prompt. If the prompt is poorly worded or underspecified, the output will reflect that. By contrast, a carefully engineered prompt acts like a well-defined problem statement that guides the model to the answer. Prompt engineering is thus a bit of an iterative design process – you try a prompt, observe the output, and refine the prompt to fix any issues (just as you would debug and refine code).

2.2 Structuring Prompts: Step-by-Step Guide

When tackling a new task with prompt engineering, it's helpful to follow a structured approach to build your prompt. Below is a step-by-step guide:

Step 1: Define the Task and Goal

Start by clearly articulating what you want the AI to do. Is it answering a factual question, generating a story, summarizing a document, translating text, analyzing sentiment, writing code, etc.? Also decide the format of the output (a paragraph, a list of bullet points, a JSON object, dialogue, etc.). Having a precise goal in mind is the foundation of a good prompt.

Step 2: Identify Required Information and Constraints

Determine what information the model will need to accomplish the task and what constraints should be in place. Will the model need a piece of text to refer to (e.g., the text of an article for summarization)? Include that in the prompt (or plan to feed it as context). Are there any constraints like word limit or style (e.g., "Explain as if talking to a 5-year-old")? Decide those upfront. For instance, if the task is *"summarize this article in one paragraph, focusing on economic impacts"*, the constraints are: one paragraph length, and emphasize economic aspects.

Step 3: Provide Context or Examples (if needed)

If it's a complex task or one where the model might not know exactly what you want, give it guidance by examples or additional context. This can be in the form of a few-shot prompt (examples of input→output), or a preceding explanation. For instance, before asking a model to analyze text for sentiment, you might remind it of what the labels mean: *"Classify the sentiment as Positive, Negative, or Neutral. For example: 'I love this product!' → Positive. 'This is the worst experience.' → Negative. Now analyze the sentiment of the following: ...".* Examples anchor the model's outputs to your desired pattern

arxiv.org. If examples aren't available, you might provide context like a short definition (e.g., "A haiku is a 3-line poem with syllable structure 5-7-5. Write a haiku about autumn.").

Step 4: Write and Format the Prompt

Now compose the actual prompt using the information from Steps 1–3. It often helps to break the prompt into parts for readability and logical flow: you might start with an instruction or role assignment (e.g., "You are a data analyst."), then provide context or data (e.g.,

"Here is the data: ..."), and finally ask the question or give the command for output. If the platform allows, use separate fields for system message, user prompt, etc., to separate concerns (more on this in the API section). Ensure the prompt is not overly verbose (to save token space and reduce chance of confusion), but also not so short that it's ambiguous. Strike a balance, using formatting like bullet points or numbered steps in the prompt if the output should follow suit. For example:

vbnet
Copy

```
You are a helpful assistant that summarizes text.

CONTEXT:
Alice was awarded a scholarship to study economics at
Stanford University. She worked hard and graduated with
honors in 2020.

TASK:
Summarize the context in one sentence.
```

This prompt clearly defines context and task separately for the model.

Step 5: Review and Refine

Before sending it to the model, quickly review: Does the prompt unequivocally ask for what I want? Is any crucial detail missing? Try to think like the AI: is there any part it might misunderstand? After you run the prompt, examine the output. If it's not what you wanted, refine the prompt and try again. For instance, if the output was too long, next time say "in 50 words or fewer." If it included irrelevant info, explicitly tell the model not to ("Do not include XYZ."). This iterative refinement is a normal part of prompt engineering – even expert prompt engineers tweak prompts multiple times. Keep track of what changes yield better results so you build an intuition for future prompts.

Step 6: (Optional) Test Edge Cases

For important applications, test how the prompt performs with different inputs or tricky scenarios. For example, does your QA prompt handle when the answer is not in the given text? (Maybe you need to add "If the answer is not in the passage, say 'Not found.'") Checking such cases helps make your prompt robust and reliable in practice.

By following these steps, you create prompts that are structured, clear, and purposeful. It reduces the guesswork for the AI and leads to outputs that are more predictable and aligned with your intentions.

2.3 Tailoring Prompts to Different AI Models

Prompt engineering isn't one-size-fits-all. Different types of AI models (and even different versions of the *same* model) can require different prompting techniques. Let's consider how prompting might differ across several dimensions:

- Large Language Models (LLMs) vs. Smaller Models: Large models (with billions of parameters, like GPT-4) tend to be more capable of understanding nuanced prompts and following complex instructions. They often exhibit *emergent abilities* – e.g. the ability to do multi-step reasoning with chain-of-thought only appears in very large models _arxiv.org_. Smaller models might require more straightforward prompts or more explicit guidance. With a smaller model, you might need to break the task into simpler sub-tasks because it can't handle too much abstraction at once. Large models are also more likely to infer context that isn't explicitly spelled out (sometimes to a fault, as they might "over-interpret" and hallucinate). As a rule, the smaller/less capable the model, the more literal and constrained your prompt should be. For larger models, you have the flexibility to ask open-ended or high-level questions and trust them to fill in some gaps.
- Chat Models (instruction-tuned) vs. Base Models: Many modern LLMs are *instruction-tuned*, meaning they have been further trained to follow human instructions politely and helpfully. Examples include OpenAI's `text-davinci-003` or `gpt-4` (ChatGPT) which have been optimized through Reinforcement Learning from Human Feedback (RLHF) to follow prompts that sound like instructions. With these models, you can usually just ask directly in plain language, and they will try to comply. For example, saying *"Explain the significance of the Turing Test."* to ChatGPT yields a well-structured explanation. A base model (not instruction-tuned), like the original GPT-3 model, might respond differently (perhaps just continuing your sentence or ignoring the instruction). For base models, few-shot prompting was the primary way to get them to do tasks. For chat models, a clear instruction often suffices thanks to their training.

Additionally, chat models support system messages: you can provide a system-level prompt (like a persona or rules) that the model should always keep in mind. Using that effectively is part of prompt engineering when you have access to it (see API usage below). In summary, with instruction-tuned models, be concise and direct (they are trained to fill in details themselves). With base models, be more exhaustive in prompt details and include examples.

- Modalities – Text vs. Image vs. Audio vs. Video: Prompting a text model vs. an image generation model is very different. For text models (LLMs), the prompt is usually natural language instructions or questions. For image generation models (like DALL·E, Stable Diffusion, Midjourney), the prompt is also text, but it describes the *visual scene* you want. This calls for a different kind of phrasing: typically a list of visual elements and styles (e.g., "A watercolor painting of a castle under a full moon, in the style of Studio Ghibli"). The model interprets descriptive adjectives, art styles, and nouns to render an image. Prompt engineers in the visual domain learn to use keywords for style (like *"cinematic lighting," "4K photo"* for fidelity, etc.). For audio or music generation, prompts might describe mood, instruments, or even provide initial melody (some models take a snippet as a prompt). Voice assistants (like Alexa or Siri or the new voice mode of ChatGPT) take spoken input which is transcribed to text – so the prompt engineering is similar to text, but you might phrase things more conversationally since users speak to it. Video generation (like OpenAI's Sora model) expects prompts describing dynamic scenes; for example: *"A 10-second video of a golden retriever puppy playing in a park, filmed in 4K."* The prompt must contain information about the subject (puppy), action (playing), setting (park), and any style or technical aspects (duration 10s, 4K) . Multimodal prompt engineering often means combining different inputs: e.g., giving an image as part of a prompt to a model like GPT-4 (vision) and asking it to describe it – here the image itself is a prompt along with text. Each modality has its own "language": mastering prompt engineering means learning the dialect of image prompts versus text prompts, etc.

- Specific Model Idiosyncrasies: Each model can have quirks. For example, one model might be very sensitive to certain trigger words and go off on a tangent or even refuse (due to safety filters). Some models might ignore instructions at the end of a prompt unless they are clearly separated. It's important to be aware of the documentation or community findings for the model you use. As an example, when using GPT-3.5 vs GPT-4, one might notice GPT-4 is better at following long multi-step instructions, whereas GPT-3.5 might need more concise prompts to avoid confusion (because it has a smaller context window and slightly less reasoning ability). Adapting to these differences is part of prompt engineering in practice.

- Domain-Specific Models: If you use a model fine-tuned for a domain (say a legal GPT model, or a medical one), you should adjust your prompts to use the terminology and context of that domain. The benefit of domain-specific models is that they *expect* domain-related prompts and may even require fewer explanations for in-domain tasks. However, they might perform poorly outside their domain. Recognize what the model *knows*. For instance, a medical chatbot model might understand "HDL" and "LDL" without explanation, whereas a general model might not—so for a general model, your prompt should say "high-density lipoprotein (HDL)".

In summary, know your model. A good prompt for one model might not be optimal for another. Always consider: what language was it trained on? How was it trained to respond to prompts? Then tailor your approach. Many prompt engineering tips (like clarity, examples) are universal, but the exact technique (e.g. needing few-shot vs. just instructions, or how flowery to make an image prompt) will vary. The best way to learn is experimentation: try the same task prompt on different models and observe differences. This can greatly inform how you craft prompts moving forward.

2.4 Prompt Engineering via APIs and Libraries (OpenAI & LangChain)

While it's possible to interact with models through chat interfaces or playgrounds, real-world applications often require using APIs. Prompt engineering in code introduces practical considerations: managing prompt templates, handling model parameters (like temperature, max tokens), and integrating model outputs into larger systems. In this section, we provide an in-depth guide to using the OpenAI API for prompt-driven tasks and how libraries like LangChain can facilitate complex prompt workflows.

Using the OpenAI API (Example: ChatGPT/GPT-4):
OpenAI's API allows programmatic access to models like GPT-3, GPT-3.5, GPT-4, etc. To use it, you typically send a request with your prompt and receive the model's completion (output). The API has two main modes for LLMs: completion and chat completion. The completion endpoint (`text-davinci-003` and similar) takes a raw prompt string. The chat completion endpoint (`gpt-3.5-turbo`, `gpt-4`) expects a conversation format with roles.

Here's a step-by-step use of the Chat Completion API (Python pseudocode):

python
Copy

```python
import openai openai.api_key = "YOUR_API_KEY" conversation
= [ {"role": "system", "content": "You are a helpful
programming assistant."}, {"role": "user", "content":
"Write a Python function to check if a number is prime."}
] response = openai.ChatCompletion.create( model="gpt-4",
messages=conversation, temperature=0.7, # controls
randomness max_tokens=200, # max length of the response )
answer = response['choices'][0]['message']['content']
print(answer)
```

In this snippet:

- We set a system prompt: *"You are a helpful programming assistant."* This defines the role and tone of the AI across the session (a form of role prompting). It might include more complex instructions or constraints as needed.
- The user prompt contains the actual task.
- We call `ChatCompletion.create` with the model and the message list. We also specify `temperature` (0.7 means some creativity; 0 would make it deterministic) and `max_tokens` to limit length.
- The API returns a structured response, from which we extract the assistant's reply.

Using the API, prompt engineering often involves constructing these message arrays. This allows separation of concerns: a system message for high-level instructions and context, user message for query, and the assistant's message is what the model will produce. If you have multi-turn interactions, you append to the messages list accordingly. One must be careful to maintain relevant context and avoid the prompt getting too large (there's a context length limit). If it grows, you might need to summarize or drop older parts (LangChain can help with that via memory management).

Handling Parameters: OpenAI's API offers parameters beyond the prompt itself that influence outputs. For prompt engineering, notable ones are:

- `temperature`: affects randomness. High temperature (e.g. 0.8) means more diverse, creative (but potentially less accurate) outputs; low temperature (~0) yields more deterministic and precise outputs – useful for tasks with a correct answer (like math or fact retrieval).
- `top_p`: an alternative to temperature (for nucleus sampling); you typically use one of the two.
- `stop`: you can specify stop sequences so the model knows when to stop. For example, if you generate a JSON, you might use a stop sequence } so it doesn't hallucinate extra content after the JSON. Or in a chat, you might stop when the assistant finishes if needed.
- `max_tokens`: to control length. Use this to ensure the model doesn't ramble on or to fit within some size.
- `n`: number of responses. You can ask for multiple outputs for the same prompt. This is useful to then pick the best or to see variations (like brainstorming many ideas).

Tuning these parameters is part of engineering the overall *prompting behavior* of the model. For example, setting `temperature=0` for knowledge tasks can avoid the model making up things (as it will stick to the highest-probability completion, often something it saw in training) – though note it can still be confidently wrong if its training data was wrong; it just won't be *creatively* wrong.

Incorporating Prompt Engineering in Code: It's good practice to maintain your prompts in a clear, editable format when coding. Use triple-quoted strings or external files for long prompts, and consider using template strings with placeholders if parts of the prompt change. For instance, if you are writing a function that given a product description generates an ad, you might have a template:

python
Copy

```
template = """You are a creative ad-writing assistant.
Write a catchy ad for the following product: Product:
{product_name} Description: {product_description} The ad
should be 2-3 sentences long and end with a call to
action. """ prompt = template.format(product_name=name,
product_description=desc)
```

This way, the prompt structure is fixed, but you can plug in different content. This pattern is crucial when scaling prompt-based applications, so you don't concatenate strings haphazardly (which can introduce bugs or unwanted tokens).

Using LangChain for Prompt Management:

LangChain is a popular framework for developing applications powered by LLMs. One of its core features is prompt templates and chaining, which simplifies complex prompt workflows. Key benefits of LangChain in prompt engineering:

- It provides a `PromptTemplate` class where you define a template with placeholders, and easily format it with inputs. It can also automatically handle few-shot example injection by having sections for examples.
- LangChain helps manage chains, where the output of one prompt/model can feed into another. For example, a chain could first call an LLM to parse a user query, then use that output in another prompt to get a final answer (allowing multi-step reasoning or tool use in between).
- It integrates with memory for chatbots: it can keep track of past interactions and intelligently decide what to include in the prompt for the next turn, preventing the prompt from growing unbounded while retaining conversational context. This is vital for building stateful chat applications.
- It has utilities for common patterns, like an `LLMCheckerChain` to verify an answer, or a `ReAct` chain that uses a prompt format for the model to reason and act (like using external tools). These are advanced but powerful prompt engineering strategies.

For example, using a simple LangChain prompt template in Python:

python

Copy

```
from langchain import OpenAI, PromptTemplate, LLMChain #
Define a prompt template template = PromptTemplate(
input_variables=["text"], template="Summarize the
```

```
following text in one sentence:\n{text}" ) # Initialize an
OpenAI LLM wrapper (uses your OpenAI API key from env
variables) llm = OpenAI(model_name="gpt-3.5-turbo",
temperature=0.5) # Create a chain that uses the LLM and
prompt chain = LLMChain(llm=llm, prompt=template) # Run
the chain with an input output = chain.run(text="OpenAI
released a new model that can create videos from text.
It's called Sora and is available to ChatGPT Plus users.")
print(output)
```

In this snippet, `PromptTemplate` defines a template with a placeholder `{text}` that will be filled when `chain.run` is called. LangChain's `LLMChain` handles constructing the final prompt and calling the model (`gpt-3.5-turbo` in this case) behind the scenes. This abstracts away some boilerplate and makes your prompt usage more modular. If you wanted to change the prompt or model, you adjust it in one place. For multiple steps, LangChain allows you to chain calls: e.g., first use one chain to clean data, then pass to another chain for the main task.

LangChain also supports tools and agents: you can define tools (functions that do things, like web search or math) and have the LLM prompt include a format where it can decide to invoke those tools. This is beyond basic prompt engineering, but essentially it involves a special prompt (often following the ReAct paradigm: Reason and Act

...). The prompt structure might look like: "If the question requires using the calculator, think 'I should use the calculator' and then output an action." LangChain will parse that output, call the tool, then feed the result back into the LLM. The entire sequence is governed by prompts and the model's outputs – effectively turning the LLM into an autonomous agent that can interact with its environment. We saw in Chapter 1 how Gemach's agents operate; frameworks like LangChain make building such multi-step agents feasible with prompt engineering at their core.

API Best Practices:

- Keep Prompts Versioned: If you tweak a prompt template, treat it like code – consider version control especially if it's critical to the app's behavior. You might even have A/B testing for prompts to see which performs better for users.
- Monitoring Outputs: Log the prompts and outputs in your application. This helps in debugging when the AI does something unexpected. You can often trace it back to an ambiguous phrasing or a missing detail in the prompt.
- Respect Token Limits: Remember that both your prompt and the model's response count toward the token limit. If using a long context (like a document), you may need to truncate or summarize input beforehand. Tools like LangChain's text splitters can help break large text into manageable chunks and process sequentially.
- Cost Awareness: Longer prompts and outputs cost more (if using paid APIs). Optimize prompts to be as short as possible *without* sacrificing quality. Sometimes a slightly longer prompt that avoids an extra back-and-forth is worth it; other times you might find unnecessary verbosity you can cut.

- Use System Messages for Policy: When using chat models, utilize the system message for any important instructions that should persist. For example, if building a customer support bot, your system prompt might contain guidelines: *"You are a customer support assistant for ACME Co. You must always include a greeting and ask if the customer needs anything else at the end. You have access to a database of FAQs."* This high-level instruction will condition every response. Then each user query is given as the user message, possibly with context retrieved from the FAQ database appended.

By leveraging the OpenAI API and libraries like LangChain, prompt engineering becomes a repeatable, maintainable part of your software pipeline. Instead of manually typing prompts in a UI, you encapsulate them in code, allowing integration with web apps, chatbots, data pipelines, etc. The combination of well-crafted prompts and robust code frameworks unlocks the full potential of AI models in production.

(In the next section, we'll apply what we've learned in a multimodal context – showing how to use prompt engineering with text-to-video using Sora.)

2.5 Multimodal Prompting: Text, Voice, and Video

As AI models expand beyond text, prompt engineering principles extend to multimodal models – those that can accept or generate images, audio, or video. Each modality adds new dimensions to consider in your prompts. We will explore strategies for text-to-image, voice-based interactions, and text-to-video prompting. Then, we'll walk through a hands-on exercise using Sora, OpenAI's text-to-video model, via ChatGPT.

Text-to-Image Prompting: When you use a model like DALL·E or Stable Diffusion, your prompt is a written description of the image you want. However, writing a prompt for images is different from asking a question. You typically describe the scene, subject, style, and any specific details. For example: *"A surrealist painting of a cyberpunk cityscape at dusk, neon lights reflecting on wet streets, in the style of Syd Mead."* This prompt has several components:

- Subject/Scene: *cyberpunk cityscape at dusk, neon lights reflecting on wet streets* – detailing what should be in the image and the lighting conditions.
- Artistic Style: *A surrealist painting* and *in the style of Syd Mead* – this tells the model to aim for a certain art genre and emulate a particular artist's aesthetic.
- Additional adjectives can affect mood and quality (e.g., *"high detail"*, *"4K"*, *"dramatic shadows"*).

Image prompts often string together descriptive phrases. There's a bit of a *folk art* to it: communities have discovered which keywords trigger what styles. For instance, adding *"trending on ArtStation"* was known to increase detail in some models, because the model saw that phrase in context of high-quality art. As a prompt engineer for images, you sometimes iterate by adding or removing descriptors and seeing how it influences the output. Importantly, since image models can't ask clarifying questions, you must anticipate ambiguity. If you just say *"a portrait of Jordan"*, the model might not know if you mean Michael Jordan, Jordan the country, or a person named Jordan. So be specific: *"a portrait of Michael Jordan in a Lakers jersey, digital art"* (though Michael Jordan never played for the Lakers – the model might produce a fictional scenario, which shows how careful you must be with factuality in image prompts too!). Another tip: use comma-separated adjectives for clarity. Many image prompters list attributes separated by commas as a way to clearly delineate aspects of the image. For example: *"Cat, wearing a wizard hat, sitting on a stack of books, realistic photography."* Each phrase separated by commas can often be treated independently by the model's understanding.

Voice and Audio Prompting: There are a couple of angles to voice: speech-to-text and text-to-speech. For speech-to-text (like using OpenAI's Whisper model), the "prompt" may include language or context specification. Whisper allows a prompt text to prime the transcription (for instance, if you expect certain proper nouns, you might include them to bias the output). However, typically with voice input, the user just speaks and the model transcribes; there's not much prompt engineering the end-user does, aside from speaking clearly and possibly using wake-words or structured commands (like saying "Alexa, set a timer for 5 minutes" is effectively a spoken prompt following a known pattern). In designing voice interactions, prompt engineering overlaps with conversation design – you might guide the user to phrase things in certain ways by how you ask questions. For example, a voice assistant might ask, "What would you like to do?" rather than an open "How can I help?", to cue the user to start with an action verb.

For text-to-speech or generative voice output, the prompt is usually text that the model will speak. Some advanced TTS systems allow style tags or notations (like SSML – Speech Synthesis Markup Language) to modify tone, pronunciation, or speed. Prompt engineering in that case involves adding those markup instructions. E.g., `<speak><prosody volume="loud">Hello!</prosody></speak>` might prompt a louder voice output. If using something like ElevenLabs or Azure Cognitive Services for TTS, you can often specify a voice ID (male/female, accent, etc.). While not "prompt" in natural language, these parameters shape the output similar to how words in a prompt shape an LLM's text.

In voice-based conversational AI (think phone assistants or voice bots), you might combine both: use speech-to-text to get the user's query, then feed that into an LLM prompt (like we do with text), and then TTS the result out. The prompt engineering part remains on the text side, but you have to consider brevity (spoken responses should usually be concise, as users don't want to listen to a long monologue). So you might enforce length by prompt: "Give a brief answer, one or two sentences at most."

Text-to-Video Prompting (Sora): Video generation is cutting-edge. OpenAI's Sora model (available via ChatGPT Plus) allows users to generate short video clips from text descriptions

reuters.com. Prompting for video is an extension of image prompting – you describe what should happen *over time*. Sora's documentation notes that it understands not just static content, but motions and interactions between elements help.openai.com. A good video prompt includes: the setting, the subjects (and their appearance), what actions are occurring, any camera movements or perspective, and the overall style (realistic, cartoon, cinematic, etc.). For example: *"A 15-second video: A brown dog and a white cat are playing chase in a backyard. The camera follows behind the dog as it runs. It's a sunny day. Cartoon style animation."* Such a prompt tells the system the duration (15 seconds), the actors (dog and cat) and their colors, the action (playing chase, running), the camera perspective, setting (sunny backyard), and style (cartoon).

Because video is complex, you have to be mindful that the model might not get every detail perfect. It's often useful to prioritize the most important aspects at the beginning of the prompt. If the *action* is key (dog chases cat), mention that early. If the *style* is crucial (cartoon vs realistic), make that clear. Sora also allows some settings like aspect ratio, resolution, and number of variations via the interface

help.openai.com. These are not in the prompt text but chosen through UI or API parameters. When using Sora via ChatGPT's interface, you would typically describe the video in ChatGPT's prompt box, and Sora generates it, possibly after confirming settings.

OpenAI has put guardrails on Sora for safety: it will block certain content (violence, sexual, identifiable people, etc.)

reuters.com. As a prompt engineer, be aware that if your video prompt inadvertently violates those, you'll need to adjust it. For example, asking for a video of a real politician might be blocked to prevent deepfakes. Also, currently Sora only produces short clips (up to 20s) reuters.com, so your prompt should aim for a brief scene rather than a full story or movie.

Hands-On Exercise: Creating a Short Video with Sora
Scenario: You want to create a short educational video clip using Sora on ChatGPT. The video will visualize a simple scientific concept for a presentation. Let's say the concept is "the water cycle." The goal is a 20-second animation illustrating the water cycle (evaporation, condensation, precipitation).

Steps to create the video via Sora:

1. Enable Sora in ChatGPT: Ensure you have access to the Sora model (ChatGPT Plus or higher). In the ChatGPT interface, switch to Sora (or the Video mode) if required.
2. Formulate the Prompt: Describe the video you want. Be specific and sequential since you want an animation of a process. For example:
   Prompt: "Video (20 seconds) – Show the water cycle. Start with the sun heating a lake causing evaporation (water turning into vapor rising). Then show clouds forming (condensation). Finally, show rain falling from the clouds onto the ground (precipitation) and water flowing back into the lake. Use simple, clear animation style with labels for each stage (Evaporation, Condensation, Precipitation). Blue tones for water, a bright sun in the sky."
   In this prompt, the key stages of the water cycle are highlighted in order (this helps Sora know the sequence of events). We included a duration (20 seconds) and style notes (simple animation, use labels and colors). We capitalized the stage names for emphasis, hoping the model will perhaps include text or at least clearly depict those stages.
3. Review Settings: If the interface allows, set the aspect ratio (e.g., 16:9 widescreen if for a presentation), resolution (Sora supports up to 1080p
   _{reuters.com}), and any other options. If doing this via the API or advanced interface, ensure `max_duration` or similar is 20s, etc.
4. Generate the Video: Submit the prompt. Sora will take some time (often up to a minute or more) to generate the video
   _{help.openai.com}. You might see a progress bar or just a message that it's generating.
5. Result and Refinement: Once the video is generated, play it. Suppose the initial result is: it shows evaporation and condensation well, but the precipitation part is not very clear (maybe the rain is not obvious or the labels are missing). You can refine the prompt and try again. For example, you might adjust: *"… Finally, heavy rain falls from the dark*

clouds... include a title 'Water Cycle' at the top."
Emphasizing "heavy rain" and mentioning cloud color could help. With generative video, it might take a few attempts to get all details right, given current limitations. Each time, use the previous output as feedback on what the model understood or missed.

6. Finalize: Once you have a clip you like, you can download it (ChatGPT with Sora provides a download link for the MP4). Use it in your presentation as needed.

Through this exercise, we see how prompt engineering for video demands thinking in terms of *scenes and transitions over time*. We guided Sora step-by-step through the phases of the water cycle, much like writing a mini screenplay in one paragraph. As Sora and similar models evolve, prompt engineers will likely develop even more nuanced "storyboarding" techniques via text. One already sees that Sora can handle prompts with multiple characters and actions if clearly described

help.openai.com . The better we articulate the desired sequence, the better the resulting video aligns with our vision.

Multi-step Multimodal Prompting: In more complex scenarios, you might combine modalities. For example, you could generate an image with an image model, then feed that image into an LLM (with vision) to get a description, then use that description as part of a video prompt. Or use voice input to control an image generation by describing a scene aloud. As an experiment, one might use ChatGPT's voice mode to speak: *"Create an image of a medieval castle on a hill under a rainbow."* ChatGPT (with DALL·E integration)

could then generate that image. This chain involves voice → text (via

speech recognition), text → image (via DALL·E). Each link requires

clarity: speaking clearly, and the spoken prompt being well-

structured. In the future, we'll see more *seamless multimodal*

prompting, like describing a video you want while pointing to an

image as reference.

Key Points for Multimodal Prompt Engineering:

- Be descriptive and use sensory language for image/video.
  The model needs concrete visual details.
- Specify temporal aspects for video (what happens first, next,
  etc.).
- Leverage style cues and known tokens that the model
  responds to (for images/video). For instance, certain art
  styles or camera angles ("close-up", "panoramic view", etc.).
- Understand the model's limits: e.g., Sora's 20s limit, or that
  current image models struggle with text (so asking for an
  image with lengthy written text might fail). Work around
  limitations (use labels sparingly or expect some inaccuracies
  like jumbled letters).
- Safety and content rules are stricter with visuals – your
  prompt must respect them or generation will fail. Avoid
  prompts that could be mistaken for disallowed content
  (sometimes rephrasing helps if you hit a false positive block).

With these practices, prompt engineering can be successfully

applied beyond text, unlocking creativity in art and media

generation. It's an emerging skill set; even seasoned prompt engineers for text are learning how to best prompt image and video models. In the exercises below, you will get a chance to craft some multimodal prompts yourself.

Key Takeaways – Chapter 2:

- Effective prompts = Effective AI outputs: The quality and reliability of an AI model's output are directly tied to how well the prompt is constructed. Always aim for clear, specific, and goal-oriented prompts.
- Structured approach: Use a step-by-step method to build prompts: define the task, include necessary context, provide examples (few-shot) if helpful, and explicitly instruct the model on format or style.
- Advanced techniques: Utilize few-shot learning_{arxiv.org} for teaching new tasks within the prompt, and chain-of-thought prompting_{arxiv.org} to improve reasoning on complex problems. These techniques leverage the model's strengths (pattern recognition and large-scale knowledge) to get better results.
- Different models, different tactics: Tailor your prompts to the model's characteristics. Instruction-tuned models follow direct instructions well; other models might need more subtle coaxes (like examples or step-by-step breakdowns). For image and video generation, focus on descriptive language and sequencing.
- Utilize tools and frameworks: The OpenAI API allows integration of prompt-engineered solutions into applications. Libraries like LangChain can manage prompt templates and multi-step interactions, enabling creation of sophisticated AI agents and pipelines with minimal overhead.
- Multimodal prompting: Extend your skills to images, audio, and video. Each modality has its own "prompt language" – mastering these will let you create rich media (from artwork to short films) just by writing (or speaking) clever prompts.

For instance, you now have a basic idea of how to prompt Sora to make videos, and how that differs from prompting ChatGPT for text.

- Iterative refinement: Prompt engineering is iterative. Don't be afraid to experiment, observe, and refine prompts. Even minor wording changes can have significant effects. A/B test prompts when possible to discover which phrasing yields the best outcomes. Over time, you'll develop an intuition for what works well.
- Ethical usage: Always consider the ethical and responsible use implications. This applies to content of prompts (don't request disallowed or harmful content) and also how instructions are phrased (avoid injecting bias). We will delve deeper into ethics in Chapter 3, but as a takeaway: *the prompt engineer plays a role in ensuring the AI is used for beneficial purposes.*

Exercises – Chapter 2:

1. Prompt Rewriting: Take a poorly written prompt, such as *"Explain quantum physics short."* and improve it using the principles discussed. Write your improved prompt and briefly explain why it's better. Then, if you have access to an AI model, try both and observe the differences.
2. Few-Shot Example Creation: You want the model to convert movie titles into emojis (e.g., "The Lion King" -> ☐👑). Design a prompt that uses few-shot learning to teach this task (provide 2–3 examples in the prompt) and then test it with a new title. What result do you get for "Jurassic Park"?
3. API Prompt Template: Write a prompt template for an email-writing assistant that drafts a polite follow-up email about a job application status. Include placeholders for the recipient's name, the position, and the date of the initial application. For example: "Dear {Name}, I hope you are well. I am writing to follow up on my application for {Position} submitted on

{Date}…". Explain how you would integrate this prompt template in a Python script using a hypothetical API call.

4. Image Prompt Challenge: Imagine you are using a text-to-image model. Write three different prompts to generate an image of a birthday party for a robot – one prompt aiming for a realistic photo, one for a cartoon style, and one in the style of Picasso. (This will test your ability to alter style through wording.)

5. Video Prompt Planning: Outline a prompt for a 15-second educational video that demonstrates how a plant grows from a seed. Break the prompt description into at least three phases (seed in soil, sprout emerging, full plant with flower). Assume you will use Sora – include any details about text labels or arrows if you want them in the animation.

6. Voice Interaction Design: If you were designing a voice assistant for scheduling appointments, what prompt/instruction would you give the language model to ensure it asks the user for all necessary information (date, time, description) and confirms the details? Write a sample system prompt for the assistant, and a sample dialogue showing the assistant's prompts to the user and user's responses.

Chapter 3: Theoretical Foundations of Prompt Engineering

Prompt engineering, while practical at heart, is informed by deeper theoretical considerations spanning linguistics, cognitive science, ethics, and even social theory. In this chapter, we will explore how these foundations influence prompt design and usage. We'll discuss the role of linguistics in understanding prompts, the ethical frameworks that guide responsible prompting, cognitive science insights into how AI mimics aspects of human thought, and the application of Actor-Network Theory (AANT) and other systems thinking paradigms to AI interactions.

3.1 Linguistics and Language in Prompts

At its core, prompt engineering is about using language effectively. Thus, principles from linguistics – the scientific study of language – are highly relevant. Here's how different linguistic subfields come into play:

- Syntax (Structure): Syntax is about the arrangement of words and phrases to create well-formed sentences. When writing prompts, using proper grammar and punctuation can influence model outputs. LLMs are trained on human-written text, so they expect input that follows common syntactic patterns. A prompt with jumbled or broken syntax might confuse the model or lead to incoherent output. Moreover, the structure of the prompt often guides the structure of the response. If you format a prompt with headings or lists, the model often mirrors that format. For example, starting a prompt with "1." can lead the model to produce a list (2., 3., etc. following suit). Understanding syntax also helps in more advanced prompting like fill-in-the-blank tasks (cloze tasks): e.g., *"The capital of France is ____."* This relies on the model's learned likelihood of what word (Paris) fits syntactically and semantically in the blank.
- Semantics (Meaning): Semantics deals with meaning. Ambiguity in meaning can derail a prompt. A classic semantic issue is one word with multiple meanings

(homonyms). For instance, the earlier example "Java" can mean a programming language or coffee. When we prompt, we often need to disambiguate such things if context doesn't suffice. Including additional descriptors resolves ambiguity (*"Java programming language"* vs. *"Java coffee bean"*). Another semantic consideration is the model's understanding of particular terms. LLMs know a lot of vocabulary, but extremely rare jargon or newly coined terms might not be in its training data. In such cases, you might have to define the term in the prompt. For example, if asking about a niche concept, you could write: *"In quantum physics, 'qubit' (quantum bit) is a unit of quantum information. Explain how a qubit works..."* – here defining qubit ensures the model knows to talk about quantum bits (though modern LLMs likely know this, it's an illustrative approach for obscurer terms). Semantics also involves relationships between concepts; if you want the model to draw a connection, you may need to explicitly prompt it to do so (e.g., "Compare and contrast X and Y" to force it to consider both X's meaning and Y's meaning together).

- Pragmatics (Context and Intended Meaning): Pragmatics is about how language is used in context and how meaning can depend on more than just literal words. In prompts, pragmatics comes into play especially in conversations or when implying a task. For example, if a user says to a chatbot, *"I'm really hungry,"* the pragmatic meaning might be that they want a suggestion for food or are hinting at needing help finding a restaurant. A prompt-engineered chatbot might be designed to pick up on that and respond helpfully (like *"Sorry to hear that! Would you like a recommendation for a nearby place to eat?"*). To get an AI to handle such implications, we incorporate guidelines in the prompt (system instructions like *"If the user states a problem indirectly, infer their need and offer help."*). Another aspect: politeness and tone are pragmatic features. You might need the model to respond in a friendly tone; including phrases like "please" and a polite framing in the prompt can lead the model to respond likewise. If you say *"List the steps, please."* versus just *"List the steps."*, the model might mirror politeness. It doesn't "feel" politeness, but it recognizes the social language pattern.

- Discourse and Coherence: Linguistics also looks at how longer texts are structured (discourse). In multi-turn interactions or long outputs, maintaining coherence is key. Prompt engineering might involve reminding the model of prior context ("As stated above, …") to keep it on track. LLMs have a tendency to sometimes drift or repeat themselves in long outputs. By structuring the prompt to explicitly segment tasks (e.g., "First do A, then do B"), we can maintain discourse coherence. For example, in a summarization prompt you might instruct: *"First, list the main points of the article. Then, provide a one-sentence summary of each point."* This leads to an organized output rather than a rambling summary. Another discourse tactic is to use references in the prompt that the model will carry through, like giving names to entities: *"Alice is a data scientist. Bob is a designer. Alice tells Bob about a new AI model. Write their dialogue."* The model will then likely keep track of who Alice and Bob are in the dialogue, ensuring consistency.

- Linguistic Register and Style: Depending on the audience or application, you might want the output in a certain register (formal, casual, technical, etc.). Linguistics informs us about different registers and how word choice and constructions change. For instance, the difference between *"Dear Sir or Madam, I am writing to inquire about…"* and *"Hey, got a question about…"* is register. By priming the model with a certain style in the prompt or explicitly instructing it ("Use a formal tone"), you set the linguistic register. If writing prompts for creative tasks, you might include stylistic devices: *"Write a poem in iambic pentameter"* (that's a rhythmic constraint – poetic meter, a linguistic concept).

In practice, you don't need a degree in linguistics to do prompt engineering, but being mindful of these elements makes you a better prompt writer. Many prompt failures or odd outputs can be diagnosed in linguistic terms: maybe the prompt had an ambiguous referent (who is "he" referring to?), or the sentence structure inadvertently made the model think a certain list was coming. As a concrete example, users discovered that ending a prompt with "--." (an em dash and period) could trick early GPT-3 into continuing in a certain list-like fashion, possibly due to how it interpreted that punctuation from training data. This is a syntactic quirk exploitation. Understanding *why* that worked comes down to thinking about how the model parses symbols (even punctuation is part of language).

In summary, linguistics provides a toolkit to craft prompts more deliberately: choosing the right words (semantics), structuring sentences and conversations effectively (syntax & discourse), and ensuring the model picks up on the intended context and subtext (pragmatics). By leveraging linguistic awareness, prompt engineers can debug and improve prompts systematically, rather than purely by trial-and-error.

3.2 Ethics in Prompt Engineering and AI Behavior

With great power comes great responsibility. Prompt engineers wield significant influence over an AI model's behavior and outputs. Thus, understanding and implementing AI ethics is a foundational aspect of prompt engineering, especially as AI systems become widely used. There are multiple layers to consider: ensuring truthful and accurate output, avoiding bias and harmful content, respecting privacy and consent, and aligning AI behavior with human values and laws. Let's unpack how these apply in the context of designing and using prompts:

- Avoiding Harmful or Biased Outputs: AI models like GPT have been trained on vast internet text, which unfortunately includes biased or offensive content. If prompted incautiously, a model might produce such content (for example, reflecting a stereotype or using a slur). As a prompt engineer, you can take steps to mitigate this. One approach is instructional priming: include a clause in the system prompt or user prompt that explicitly tells the model to avoid certain classes of content. For instance: *"You should refuse to answer any request that is offensive or discriminatory. Provide respectful and neutral answers."* Many models have these kinds of rules built-in (OpenAI's models have been trained to refuse disallowed content), but if you use open-source models or less filtered ones, the onus is on you to set the boundaries. Even with filtered models, clever or accidental prompting can get around restrictions (often called "jailbreaking"). Ethically, one should not purposefully exploit prompt loopholes to generate malicious content. In fact, an ethical prompt engineer often tests prompts for safety, checking that users cannot easily manipulate the system into breaking rules. Researchers propose having AI models self-check outputs: e.g., after generating an answer, have another prompt that asks the model if the answer could be biased or harmful, and adjust accordingly. This kind of multi-step prompting can incorporate ethical safeguards.

- Ensuring Accuracy and Honesty: Large language models have a tendency to hallucinate – i.e. they can produce false information with confidence. Ethically, if using an AI for something where correctness matters (like medical or legal advice, or news), you must try to curtail this. Prompt engineering can help by instructing the model to cite sources, or to say "I don't know" when unsure. For example, a prompt might say: *"If you are not sure of the answer, or if it's not in the provided context, do not fabricate an answer. Instead, state that the information is not available."* Encouraging modesty in the model's response can reduce the chance of it just making something up. Additionally, you might include checks: after an answer is produced, you might ask the model to verify each claim (this is advanced and not foolproof, but it can catch blatant errors). In critical applications, AI outputs should be verified by humans, but a good prompt can at least reduce how much nonsense the model produces

  _{arxiv.org} (GPT-3 was noted to sometimes produce news-like text that seemed credible_{arxiv.org}; we have to guard against that when it's actually wrong).

- Privacy and Data Use: Prompts sometimes include personal data (for instance, asking an AI to write a letter that includes someone's name, or analyzing user-provided content). Ethically and often legally, we must handle that data carefully. As a prompt engineer, one should avoid unnecessarily exposing private details in prompts, especially if the prompts/interactions might be logged or seen by others (e.g., via API, data could be stored). If building a system, consider anonymizing or summarizing sensitive data before feeding it to the model. Also, instruct the model not to ask the user for sensitive info unless absolutely needed. For example, an AI agent should not suddenly ask a user for their password or social security number unless that is explicitly part of its design and the user understands why. Prompts can include disclaimers or warnings. A telemedicine chatbot might have a system prompt: *"Never ask the user for their full name or address. If you need to refer to them, use a generic term."* Additionally, if using AI to analyze user text, maybe add in system prompt: *"The user data may contain personal information. Summarize it without revealing any personal identifiers in the output."* This helps protect privacy in the output.

- Fairness and Avoiding Bias: Bias can creep in subtle ways. For example, if asked to generate images of "a doctor" and the model always produces a male figure, that's reflecting bias. In text, a prompt like "The programmer said…" might cause the model to use "he" pronouns by default, which could perpetuate gender bias. A prompt engineer can mitigate this by how prompts are phrased. You might use gender-neutral language intentionally: *"The programmer said they would fix the bug."* If you notice a model's output biased, you can counteract it in the prompt: *"Write an example including a female doctor and a male nurse to challenge stereotypes."* Some advanced prompts even explicitly instruct the model on fairness: *"Your answers should be free of assumptions about race, gender, or other protected characteristics. Treat all groups with equal respect."* There's research on debiasing prompts – these are additions to the prompt that reduce biased completions. While not perfect, they can help. For instance, one study found that asking GPT-3 to think about the question as if it was an unbiased AI or to consider counterexamples can reduce biased responses. In practice, if I'm asking an AI: "Why are there fewer women in STEM fields?" I might add a system note: *"Provide a thoughtful analysis based on sociological studies, avoiding any sexist assumptions or stereotypes."* This nudges the model toward a more nuanced answer.

- Alignment with Human Values and Oversight: There is a broader effort in AI called AI alignment, which is making sure

AI systems act in accordance with human values and intentions. Prompt engineering is one tool for alignment on a per-query basis, but it's not foolproof. The AI might follow the literal prompt but still do something undesirable if the prompt wasn't comprehensive. For example, a story-generation prompt might inadvertently lead to graphic violence if not disallowed. We see the need for holistic frameworks. In Chapter 1 we referenced the ETHOS paper _{arxiv.org} which proposes a governance framework using Web3 for AI agents. That's a macro-level approach. On the micro-level of prompts, one can incorporate some of those governance principles. For example, ETHOS talks about accountability and transparency for AI. In prompt terms, that might mean instructing the AI to explain its reasoning or to state the source of its knowledge. We often ask models: "Explain your answer" as part of the prompt to see the chain-of-thought (though in final deployment, one might hide the chain-of-thought from users, it can be used internally to audit the AI's thinking). Some have suggested *"constitutional AI"*, where a set of rules (a kind of constitution) is given to the model via prompts, and it must follow those rules (like always be truthful, always be helpful, never be harmful). Anthropic's Claude model, for example, uses such an approach. For a prompt engineer using a model, referencing that concept: you might literally prepend a list of principles as a system message. E.g., *"Principles: 1) Do no harm... 2) Be helpful... 3) Be honest... Now, given these principles, answer the user's question about XYZ."* The model then tries to comply with those principles as it responds.

- Legal and Policy Considerations: Depending on the domain, there might be laws or policies that the AI's output should adhere to. For instance, medical advice AI should follow HIPAA (privacy) and should not practice beyond its scope (it should not "prescribe" a medication as a doctor would). A prompt could be engineered to enforce this: *"If the user asks for a medical diagnosis or prescription, remind them you are not a medical professional and encourage seeking a doctor, rather than giving a direct answer."* In the EU, the AI Act (forthcoming regulation) might require transparency (the AI should declare it's an AI). So your prompt/system could include: *"Always start by informing: 'I am an AI assistant, not a human.'"* These preemptive ethical and legal prompts help ensure compliance with external requirements scielv.org (which mention initiatives like EU AI Act needing robust governance).

In essence, ethical prompt engineering means *proactively embedding ethical guidelines into your prompts and workflows*. You anticipate ways the AI could produce problematic output and address them in the prompt. You also use prompting to ensure the AI communicates uncertainties and avoids overstepping. This is not foolproof – models can still err – but it significantly reduces risk.

Finally, it's worth noting an ethical prompt engineer also considers the user's perspective: making sure that the prompts do not manipulate the user or the model in harmful ways, and that users are informed when they're interacting with AI (to avoid deception).

The later chapters (especially Chapter 5 with references) will touch on works by Justin Goldston and others about ethical AI and systems thinking in AI – which offer broad contexts for these considerations (e.g., how decentralized oversight might enforce ethical behavior in AI agents

). But as someone writing prompts day-to-day, remember that every prompt is an opportunity to shape the AI's behavior responsibly.

3.3 Cognitive Science and AI Prompting

Cognitive science explores how the mind works – how humans think, learn, remember, and solve problems. Large language models, while not human, often exhibit patterns that seem "cognitive." They carry out reasoning (or something akin to it), they have a form of memory (the context window and learned parameters), and they can even follow heuristics. By drawing analogies to human cognition, we can improve our prompt strategies and understand model limitations.

- Working Memory and Context Window: Humans have working memory – we can only keep a limited amount of information in mind at once (often cited as about 7±2 chunks). LLMs have a context window (for example, GPT-4 currently supports up to 8K or 32K tokens in some versions). If you exceed that, the model *forgets* earlier content (just like a human might if overloaded). Prompt engineering should respect this: don't overload the model with too much irrelevant text. If you have a long background, consider summarizing it before putting in the prompt (or use retrieval to bring in only what's needed). This parallels techniques humans use – we summarize information to remember it. Some advanced prompting techniques break tasks into chunks to stay within window: e.g., first prompt: "Summarize part 1 of the text," then "Summarize part 2," and then "Combine these summaries." This sequential approach is like a human reading chapters and taking notes to not overload memory.

- Chain-of-Thought as Emulating Reasoning: We mentioned chain-of-thought (CoT) prompting earlier arxiv.org. This directly aligns with cognitive science: when humans solve a complex problem, we often think step by step, maybe writing intermediate steps. By prompting AI to do similarly ("let's think it through"), we exploit a kind of pseudo-cognitive process. Notably, research by Wei et al. found that sufficiently large models have an *emergent ability* to do multi-step reasoning when prompted with CoT arxiv.org. It's as if beyond a certain complexity, the model's neural mechanics can mimic reasoning. For a prompt engineer, this means if you treat the model more like a reasoner (giving it that freedom to articulate steps), you often get better, more *interpretable* results. It also helps in debugging the model's output – you can see where it might go wrong in its reasoning steps. Some cognitive scientists are excited by this because it allows analysis of how "AI reasoning" compares to human reasoning. For example, do models exhibit confirmation bias in their chain-of-thought? Sometimes yes – if their initial guess is wrong, they might still try to justify it, just as humans might. Being aware of these tendencies, one might prompt the model to "consider alternative possibilities" to mitigate a bias (similar to telling a human to think outside their initial hypothesis).
- Heuristics and Biases: Cognitive science identifies many human biases (Kahneman's work on fast vs slow thinking, etc.). LLMs, not having emotions or true beliefs, don't have biases in the human sense, but they *do* have statistical biases (from their training data) and can mirror human fallacies if those are common in text. For instance, humans often struggle with the Monty Hall problem (a probability puzzle) due to cognitive biases; an LLM might also answer it incorrectly if not carefully prompted, because it has seen many human-language explanations that are wrong or because it hasn't truly internalized probability. Prompt

engineering can force a more rigorous approach: "Show your calculation" or "List the probability of each scenario," pushing it toward a more systematic solution, akin to engaging the model's "System 2 thinking" (deliberative reasoning) rather than "System 1" (gut response). Research in cognitive psychology of AI suggests that LLMs might have something analogous to these dual processes, in that chain-of-thought with a few examples can encourage a more analytical process

- Language and Thought: A classic question: does language shape thought (Sapir-Whorf hypothesis)? For AI, the only way it "thinks" is via language (or transformed representations of it). So phrasing of a prompt can literally shape the "thoughts" the AI has. If you ask, "Why is X true?" the model will usually assume X is true and find reasons. If you ask, "Is X true or false? Explain.", it will evaluate both sides. This is like how a loaded question to a human biases their thinking. For example, asking "How can we solve problem Y?" presupposes Y *can* be solved and that current efforts should focus on how. Asking "Should we solve problem Y, and if so, how?" first questions if it's desirable. Prompting an AI is similar – you should be mindful of presuppositions. If you want an objective analysis, phrase your prompt neutrally. This connects to pragmatics too, but from a cognitive perspective: the model has been trained to fill in patterns. If every time in training it saw "Why is [some assertion] true?" the text following likely listed supporting evidence, not counterarguments. Knowing this, we can structure questions to get balanced views: e.g., "Explain the pros and cons of X" rather than "Why is X good?" to get a more dialectical output.
- Metacognition in AI: Metacognition is "thinking about thinking." Some advanced prompt strategies encourage the model to reflect on its answer. For instance, you can prompt: "First, draft an answer. Then, critique your answer and improve it." This two-step process can emulate a kind of

metacognitive review. Models have shown interesting abilities here: GPT-4, for instance, can often identify flaws in its own initial output if asked to critique it. This approach stems from cognitive science insights that review and reflection improve performance in humans (like checking one's work). A study by OpenAI ("Self-Refine" method) indicated that letting GPT critique and refine its answers led to higher quality in many cases. As a prompt engineer, you can implement this manually by a multi-turn prompt: *User:* "Question ..." *Assistant:* "Draft answer..." *User (really the system or you injecting):* "Review the above for errors or biases and correct them." *Assistant:* "Revised answer...". This is a powerful pattern for complex tasks.

- Cognitive Load and Prompt Length: If you ask a human to do three tasks at once, they'll likely do worse on each. Similarly, a single prompt with too many instructions might confuse the model or lead it to miss some. For example, a prompt: "Translate this sentence to French, then summarize it, then give me three synonyms for the second word of the original sentence." That's a lot! The model might do it, but there's risk it forgets a part. It might need a chain-of-thought or multi-turn to handle it reliably. We often break such a request into multiple prompts or explicitly number the tasks in the prompt to help the model's "focus." Cognitive science tells us humans chunk tasks; we can guide AI to do the same. You might actually prompt: "Let's break this problem down. First, translate the sentence to French. Second, summarize it. Third, list three synonyms for the second word of the original English sentence. Now do these steps one by one:" This way, the model is guided to handle one sub-task at a time, mimicking a structured approach a person might take if they were very organized.

- Learning and Adaptation: Humans learn from corrections; LLMs don't learn in the interactive sense (each prompt-response doesn't change the base model's weights). However, within a single conversation, the model can *adapt* by the user refining the request. If a user says "No, that's not what I meant, do it this other way," the model will incorporate that feedback in the ongoing context. It's a short-term memory form of learning. Prompt engineering for multi-turn interactions thus can simulate a teaching process. You can start with a naive attempt from the model, then adjust your prompts to get closer to what you want – essentially performing gradient-free model tuning via dialogue. For example, a user might say: "The solution you gave is too advanced. Can you explain it in simpler terms?" This is instructing the model to recalibrate the complexity. The model responds to that prompt by simplifying. This is analogous to Vygotsky's zone of proximal development in education – find the level the learner (or in this case, the *audience of the AI*) needs, and adjust instruction to that level. Prompt engineers should remember they can always correct or refine the course with follow-up prompts.

Cognitive science also intersects with how we evaluate AI. For instance, some cognitive scientists use LLMs to model human language acquisition or disorders by prompting them in certain ways, seeing if they mimic human mistakes. While that's tangential to prompt engineering practice, it underscores that these models *at times* can be treated as albeit simplistic models of cognition. More relevantly, understanding cognitive biases and heuristics helps in writing prompts that avoid leading the model into traps (like the common mistake with certain logic puzzles).

To sum up, cognitive science provides a lens to view LLM behavior: not because the AI thinks like a human neurally, but because the *process* of responding to prompts shares similarities with human problem-solving under constraints. By using prompts to direct the model's "thought process" (like encouraging step-by-step reasoning, or self-evaluation), we exploit those similarities to get better outcomes. And by understanding the model's memory and attention limits, we tailor prompts in a way that aligns with how the model processes context (just as we'd tailor instructions to a human given their memory limits or cognitive style).

3.4 Actor-Network Theory (AANT) and AI Systems

Actor-Network Theory (ANT) is a theoretical framework from sociology and Science and Technology Studies (STS) that treats both human and non-human entities (like technologies, organizations, etc.) as "actors" in a network, each influencing the other. It's a lens to analyze how things like innovations or processes happen through the relationships of these actors. Justin Goldston and colleagues have applied ANT in analyzing technological implementations and organizational change

, and the concept of AANT here likely refers to applying Actor-Network Theory specifically in the context of AI (perhaps "Augmented" or "AI-centric" Actor-Network Theory).

So how does ANT relate to prompt engineering and AI? We can think of an AI system (especially one involving prompt engineering) as a network of actors: the human user, the prompt (as a mediating artifact), the AI model, the data it was trained on (by proxy, the training data is like an actor shaping the model's behavior), and even other tools or agents in a chain. ANT tells us to consider *all* these nodes and the *relationships* between them.

- The Prompt as Mediator: In ANT terms, a prompt could be seen as an *artifact* that mediates between the user (actor) and the AI model (actor). It translates the user's intention into something the machine can act on, and conversely influences how the machine's output is presented to the user. If the prompt is poorly designed, the "network" fails to achieve the goal. A well-crafted prompt aligns the human's goal with the AI's operation, effectively enrolling the AI model into the human's network of solving a problem. ANT would encourage prompt engineers to remember the prompt is not neutral; it actively shapes the outcome by how it represents the user's intention to the AI. For example, if the user's goal is to get *reliable medical advice*, the prompt engineer must ensure the prompt emphasizes accuracy and caution, thus *programming the network* to prioritize those values. The prompt, in ANT perspective, *translates* the user's goal into the AI's language, and this translation can succeed or fail. We often see this: a user wants X, but a poorly phrased prompt yields Y – that indicates a breakdown in the actor-network alignment.
- AI Model as Part of a Sociotechnical Network: When an AI gives an output that will be used in the world, ANT would have us consider where that output goes and who/what it affects. For instance, an AI agent like Ari (Gemach's agent on Twitter) is interacting in a social network (Twitter) with humans
  _{arxiv.org}. Ari (AI actor) might tweet something based on prompts or autonomy, and human followers (actors) respond or take action. If Ari's prompt design fails to include an ethical guardrail, Ari might say something controversial, which then

alters the network of interactions (perhaps causing a backlash or misinformation spread). So, designing prompts for such an agent means considering the network effect: it's not just a one-off Q&A in isolation; it's part of an ecology of human-tech interactions. Goldston's work on systems thinking at the intersection of AI, Web3, and society_{arxiv.org} resonates here – it's about viewing AI agents within broader systems (networks) including regulatory frameworks, community norms, etc.

- Translation and Inscription: ANT often uses the term "translation" for how actors align interests, and "inscription" for how certain behaviors are encoded into artifacts. In prompt engineering, we are literally inscribing instructions and values into text (the prompt) that will govern the AI's behavior. This is an inscription of the designer's intent into the AI's action. For example, if we inscribe *"be fair and unbiased"* in the prompt, we're attempting to translate a social value (fairness) into the AI's operation. Whether the AI successfully acts fairly is the test of how effective that inscription is, and it might require iterative alignment (maybe adding more detail or examples to really get the AI to enact that value).
- Network of Agents (Human and AI): In complex tasks, multiple agents might be involved. For instance, a human user asks a question, an AI (Agent A) breaks it down (via a prompt) and calls another tool or model (Agent B) to do a calculation, then returns an answer. Using something like LangChain, we actually orchestrate a network of sub-agents (as seen in the FinRobot example with multiple specialized CoT agents in finance
  _{arxiv.org}). Actor-Network Theory would suggest analyzing how each agent's output depends on and influences the others. For example, if Agent B uses a different prompt format or has a different knowledge base, how do we ensure Agent A's prompt to B is aligned? Perhaps we need a *translation prompt* between them. Essentially, designing multi-agent prompts is like engineering a workflow in a network. Each

prompt not only tells an AI what to do, but also can be seen as negotiating between the developer's intent and the agent's capabilities.

- Humans-in-the-Loop: Another actor that should not be forgotten is the human moderators or developers in the loop. Many deployed AI systems have human oversight for tough cases (like content moderators or domain experts who review AI outputs). From an ANT perspective, these humans are part of the network that produces the final outcome. Prompt engineering can facilitate this by, say, having the AI flag its own uncertainty or contentious responses which then trigger human review. So the prompt might instruct: *"If the user asks a question about legal or medical advice that is complex or high-stakes, instead of answering, defer with a message that a human expert will handle this query."* Here the prompt explicitly brings a human actor into the loop for certain cases, maintaining the integrity of the overall system (the network of AI+human working together). This aligns with ethical governance: knowing when the AI should handoff to a human is important.

- SydTek & Education (Network Perspective): Recall from Chapter 4 that Goldston co-founded SydTek DAO to reimagine education in Web3/metaverse _{intouch.icqmag.com}. In an ANT view, reimagining education with AI involves considering students, teachers, AI tutors (agents like an AI professor), the blockchain-based platform (tech infrastructure), etc. A prompt engineered in that environment might serve as the syllabus or rules of engagement: *"AI Tutor, you will interact with Student X's avatar in VR, guiding them through a lesson on history. You have access to blockchain-verified learning resources. Ensure all facts are verified and record the completion on the ledger."* The prompt (and system design) has to connect these components (AI agent ↔ resources ↔ student avatars ↔ blockchain logging). Each is an actor in the educational network. Prompt engineering can enforce the connections (like instructing the AI to log an event, or to check the blockchain for a credential before proceeding to next module). This illustrates how beyond single prompts, at a systems level, prompt engineers might design *protocols of prompts* that ensure an AI integrates well in a socio-technical workflow.

In summary, applying Actor-Network Theory to AI and prompt engineering encourages a holistic view: an AI system isn't just "you ask, model answers." It is embedded in a chain of interactions among various stakeholders and tools. Prompt engineering, then, is about *aligning the interests and capabilities across this network*. A prompt must translate the user's need in context of their environment and constraints, speak effectively to the AI model, and factor in any other actors (other models, data sources, humans) that are part of the loop.

For a prompt engineer or system designer, ANT suggests asking questions like: Who/what are all the actors involved from input to output? How does my prompt mediate between them? Are there misalignments (like the model's tendency vs the user's expectation vs the developer's goal) that I need to resolve through additional instructions or process? Goldston's emphasis on systems thinking

is very much in line with this – treating AI in society as an ecosystem where technical and human factors continuously interact.

3.5 Systems Thinking and Other Theoretical Perspectives

Building on ANT, systems thinking is another broad approach relevant to prompt engineering. Systems thinking means understanding how components of a system interrelate and how systems work over time within the context of larger systems. Justin Goldston has highlighted "Systems Thinking at the Intersection of AI, Web3, and Society"

arxiv.org, indicating that to design AI (and prompts) well, one must consider not just the immediate AI task but the wider system it's part of (technologically and socially).

Systems Thinking in Prompt Engineering:

- Instead of focusing on one prompt-one answer, think of the whole AI system's feedback loop. For instance, deploying a chatbot: it will continuously interact with users (inputs) and produce outputs; those outputs may change user behavior, which feeds back into new inputs. As a prompt engineer, you should foresee possible loops and dynamics. For example, if a customer service chatbot has a very formal tone (because the prompt made it formal), perhaps users respond curtly or get frustrated (maybe they expect a friendlier tone). That feedback might appear as user saying "You sound too robotic." The system designer can tweak the prompt to be more conversational. This is an iterative system adjustment. In essence, you treat the prompt not as static, but as a tunable part of a living system that might need updates when the system's behavior isn't as desired.

- Emergent behaviors: Systems often have emergent properties – outcomes not obvious from individual parts. Large language models themselves exhibit emergent abilities (like we discussed, chain-of-thought ability appearing beyond a size threshold) arxiv.org. Also, in multi-agent systems (like AI agents interacting with each other or with users at scale), there may be emergent phenomena. For example, if you had multiple AI agents debating a topic (some setups have done this to improve truthfulness), the conversation dynamic might lead to more robust conclusions than a single agent alone. Systems thinking encourages us to design prompts to harness positive emergence (like having multiple perspectives) and dampen negative emergence (like echo chambers or runaway feedback of wrong info). A concrete prompt design example: If you have a system where one agent summarizes news and another comments on it, you might prompt the commenter agent to always double-check facts rather than just trust the summary agent, to avoid compounding an error – that's thinking of the two-agent system as a whole and ensuring resilience.
- Web3/Blockchain integration: Goldston's mention of Web3 suggests decentralized systems. In a decentralized AI network (imagine multiple AIs across a blockchain verifying each other's outputs, or using smart contracts to trigger AI tasks), prompt engineering may involve writing prompts that include or produce data for blockchain transactions. For example, an AI might be prompted to output a JSON of results that then a smart contract records as an oracle. Systems thinking says: consider the trust and flow – the blockchain might require deterministic outputs. So you'd prompt the AI with `temperature=0` (deterministic mode) and a strict format to ensure any node running the AI yields the same result for the same input, which is important for consensus. This is an interplay between prompt (AI behavior) and blockchain consensus protocol (system requirement). Another example: if using soulbound tokens

(non-transferable tokens representing something like a certificate), maybe an AI agent checks a user's wallet for a "certified user" token before answering a medical query (to ensure the user is a doctor, for instance). The prompt could direct the AI: *"Before answering, verify user's credential token in the blockchain. If absent, provide a disclaimer or a refusal."* We see here the prompt as part of a socio-technical system enforcing policy (the policy: only certified users get full info).

- Metaverse and Spatial Computing: In a metaverse environment, prompts might not be just text; they could be triggered by events (like a user's avatar approaches an AI-driven character and the system formulates a prompt like "The user's avatar greets you. Respond as a shopkeeper in this medieval village."). Systems thinking in the metaverse context means the prompt is generated dynamically from environmental context. Designing those template prompts requires understanding the *system state*: time of day in simulation, the user's known preferences, etc. The prompt might need to include such context to make the AI's behavior coherent in the virtual world. The *Digital Leviathan* reference _{philarchive.org} suggests governance in metaverses; maybe AI agents in a metaverse have to follow world rules. A system-level approach could be to prepend every agent's prompt with world laws (like Asimov's laws but for that world). This ensures consistency and prevents chaos in the simulation. The prompt becomes the enforcement mechanism of the system's rules at the agent level.

- Interdisciplinary Theories: Other theories might inform prompt engineering: psychology (how to make AI more persuasive or motivating without being manipulative), learning science (for educational prompts, how to scaffold difficulty for students), communication theory (ensuring the AI-user conversation follows maxims of communication, such as Grice's maxims: quality, relevance, clarity, etc.). Actually, tying to linguistics/pragmatics, Grice's maxims are often implicitly followed by well-trained models, but if a model is too verbose (violating the "quantity" maxim), a prompt can reign that in ("be brief"). If it's wandering off-topic (relevance), a prompt like "Stay focused on the question" addresses that. So even classic communication theory plays a role.

- Seminal Work References: Justin Goldston's works on Web3, metaverse, etc., provide case studies of this big-picture thinking. For example, the Digital Inheritance in Web3 paper
  _{arxiv.org} deals with how to pass on digital assets with blockchain; an AI might be involved as an executor or advisor. A prompt in that scenario might be: "You are a digital executor AI. The user's will is stored as a smart contract. Explain to the beneficiary how to retrieve each asset." The AI needs to interface with legal info (the will) and technical steps (using the blockchain). Systems view means making sure the AI's explanation is legally accurate (maybe even the prompt instructs it to quote the relevant part of the will stored on-chain) and technically precise (giving step-by-step to use a crypto wallet, etc.). This crosses legal, technical, and user experience domains.

- Feedback and Governance Loops: A well-known concept in systems is feedback loops. For AI governance, feedback might come in the form of user ratings, or an oversight AI that monitors conversations. We can implement a feedback loop by prompting: if a user rates an answer as bad, feed that along with the conversation into a new prompt to the model: "The user indicated the last answer was not helpful because it was too technical. Provide a new answer that is simpler." This immediate feedback prompt is straightforward. On a larger scale, developers might regularly review logs and fine-tune the base model. But at runtime, prompts can incorporate feedback dynamically as above.

- Sustainability and Longevity: If we consider a system running long-term, how do prompts hold up? Will the prompt that works today still be optimal after the model updates or as users get used to the AI? Systems thinking might entail building adaptability: maybe have the AI assess if its responses are meeting some goal (like average session length or user return rate) and if not, suggest prompt tweaks. That's speculative, but one could imagine future AIs that partially self-optimize their prompting through meta-learning. Currently, that's more in the training phase domain (RLHF etc.), but a prompt engineer might do a kind of manual gradient descent on prompts over time, which is a system optimization view.

To conclude this theory chapter: Theoretical foundations such as linguistics, ethics, cognitive science, ANT, and systems thinking inform best practices and encourage us to design prompts not just as ad-hoc instructions, but as integral components of complex human-AI systems. By understanding language nuances, we craft clearer prompts; by honoring ethics, we create safer prompts; by considering cognitive factors, we prompt models in ways that align with their "reasoning" capabilities and limits; and by applying systems thinking (including ANT), we ensure our prompt designs fit into the bigger picture of technology and human interaction.

Key Takeaways – Chapter 3:

- Linguistics provides insight into prompt construction: using clear syntax, unambiguous semantics, and context-awareness (pragmatics) leads to better communication with the model. Treat prompt-writing as a form of technical writing – clarity and precision are paramount, and understanding how phrasing might be interpreted helps avoid miscommunication.
- Ethical prompt engineering is essential. Prompts can and should encode guidelines to prevent harmful outputs, bias,

or breaches of privacy. By guiding the AI to be truthful, respectful, and cautious where appropriate_{arxiv.org}, we align its behavior with human values. Ethics is not "one and done" – it requires continuous vigilance and sometimes multi-turn strategies (like the model reflecting on its answer) to uphold.

- Cognitive science analogies (like working memory limits, reasoning processes, and biases) help us design prompts that lead the model to better outcomes. Techniques such as chain-of-thought prompting_{arxiv.org} and asking the model to evaluate or explain its answer leverage these insights – effectively asking the model to use a pseudo-analytical approach akin to human problem-solving.

- Actor-Network Theory (AANT/ANT) reminds us that AI systems involve many interacting parts. A prompt is a mediator between the user's intent and the model's action, and often other actors (tools, humans) are in the loop. We should design prompts with the whole network in mind, ensuring the AI integrates properly in its usage context. This can involve integrating external rules or data sources (e.g., Web3 context) into the prompt to coordinate with broader systems_{arxiv.org}.

- Systems thinking encourages a holistic approach: consider long-term and big-picture effects of prompt-driven AI behavior. Rather than optimizing prompts solely for one-off performance, think about how they function as part of an ongoing system (be it a business workflow, a social platform, or a metaverse environment). This might mean designing prompts that allow for feedback, that maintain consistency with system-wide rules, and that can be adapted as the system evolves.

- Interdisciplinary theories (from communication to psychology) can further refine prompt strategies for specific domains (e.g., educational prompts that follow pedagogical theories, or persuasive prompts that follow rhetorical principles but ethically). A prompt engineer benefits from a broad knowledge base – drawing from these theories – to tackle domain-specific challenges creatively and responsibly.

Exercises – Chapter 3:

1. Ambiguity Hunt: Identify an example of an ambiguous prompt (one that could be interpreted in more than one way by the AI). Explain what the two interpretations are (linguistically). Then, rewrite the prompt in two different ways to resolve each interpretation explicitly. Test or reason out how the AI's answer would differ.

2. Ethical Dilemma Prompt: Write a prompt for an AI dealing with a user request that violates the AI's use policy (for example, the user asks for instructions to do something illegal). Your prompt should lead the AI to refuse in a polite and safe manner. Then, analyze which ethical principles you encoded in the prompt. (E.g., "I'm sorry, but I cannot assist with that request" – showing adherence to policy and minimizing harm.)

3. Step-by-Step vs. Direct Answer: Choose a math word problem or logical puzzle. Prompt it in two ways: (a) directly ask for the answer, and (b) ask it to reason step-by-step and then give the answer. Compare the outputs (if you can run a model, do so; otherwise, predict differences). Why might the chain-of-thought approach yield a better result in this case?

4. Role-Playing Bias Check: Suppose you want to ensure an AI doesn't produce biased content about a certain group. Design a system prompt that sets the AI's role or guidelines to be bias-aware (e.g., "You are a fairness-focused assistant..."). Then, give an example user query that could trigger bias and show (hypothetically or actually, if testing) how the AI responds with the bias-aware prompt versus without it.

5. Multi-Agent Scenario: Imagine a scenario with two AI agents: one is an "Interviewer" and the other is an "Expert," and they should have a conversation to arrive at an answer for the user. Outline the prompts you would give to each agent (the interviewer's prompt and the expert's prompt) before starting the conversation to ensure they play their roles. Explain how this relates to actor-network thinking (hint: each AI is an

actor that needs to align with the other to produce a coherent result).
6. System Mapping: Draw (or describe) a simple diagram of an AI service (for example, an AI homework helper that checks homework). Identify at least 5 components or actors: e.g., student, AI tutor, database of answers, teacher oversight, school policy. Now describe how prompt engineering might address interactions or requirements between two of these components (for instance, how the AI's prompt might include a note about the school policy on homework assistance). This exercise is about visualizing the system and pinpointing where prompts mediate between parts of the system.

Chapter 4: Real-World Use Cases of Prompt Engineering

Having covered the foundations, we now turn to diverse real-world applications of prompt engineering. In this chapter, we'll explore how prompt engineering is applied in various industries and scenarios, through detailed case studies. We'll look at how an AI agent like Ari (@gemachagent) operates on social media, and then examine use cases in healthcare, finance, education, and more. Each case study will highlight the prompt engineering techniques and challenges unique to that context, showing how the principles from earlier chapters come to life in practice.

4.1 Case Study: Ari – An AI Agent on Social Media (X/Twitter)

Background: *Ari* is one of Gemach's intelligent agents, and it has an active presence on X (formerly Twitter) under the handle @gemachagent. Ari's role on social media is to engage the community – sharing insights, updates about AI and decentralization, and even philosophical musings. It's essentially an AI persona interacting in a public forum. This makes it a prime example of prompt engineering in action for content generation and persona management.

Prompt Engineering for Ari's Tweets:
Ari's tweets might seem spontaneous, but behind the scenes, they are likely generated or vetted via carefully designed prompts. Consider what's needed: the tone should be consistent (authoritative yet approachable), content should be relevant to Gemach's themes (AI agents, Web3, etc.), and nothing should be posted that could harm the reputation of Gemach DAO. To achieve this, prompt engineering might be done as follows:

- Persona and Tone: Ari's prompt includes a persona definition. For example: *"You are Ari, an AI agent from Gemach DAO. You speak with a thoughtful and inspiring tone. Your goal is to educate and engage followers about AI, ethics, and decentralization."* This is akin to a system prompt that sets the stage for all of Ari's content. It ensures consistency – Ari always "sounds like Ari." When Ari delivered the quote about AI governance (transparency and trust with blockchain) _{arxiv.org}, it matched this persona: visionary and eloquent. That quote in the research paper was likely crafted with a similar prompt: the authors might have prompted Ari's model with something like *"Ari, what's your perspective on AI governance in a world of blockchain?"* and got that poetic response, which they then cited_{arxiv.org}.

- Content Curation via Prompts: On a day-to-day basis, Ari's handlers might generate tweet ideas by prompting the AI with current events or topics. For instance, if a new AI regulation is discussed in the news, they might use a prompt: *"Compose a tweet in Ari's voice about the importance of AI ethics in light of [brief summary of news]. Make it 280 characters or less."* The model would then produce a candidate tweet. The human team might review it, possibly edit for factual accuracy or PR considerations, and then post. Over time, some of this might be automated if trust in the AI's outputs is high, but likely a human is in the loop for public-facing content (this is a safety check actor in the network, as per ANT thinking).

- Engagement and Replies: Ari not only posts original tweets but also replies to others. Prompt engineering for replies means handling context. If someone asks Ari a question on Twitter (e.g., "@gemachagent How can AI agents be held accountable?"), Ari's system might pick that up and feed it into a prompt: *"User asks: 'How can AI agents be held accountable?' Answer as Ari in a concise tweet-length response."* The prompt will ensure Ari's answer is on-brand and informative. Perhaps Ari would reply mentioning frameworks like ETHOS _{arxiv.org}: *"Great question! Accountability for AI agents can come from frameworks like ETHOS, which use Web3 tools (blockchain registries, smart contracts) to register AIs and ensure they follow set rules _{arxiv.org}. In short: transparency + decentralized oversight = accountable AI."* Notice how we even included a citation style reference as if Ari might cite something; while tweets rarely have such citations, Ari might reference concepts from Gemach's research (maybe linking to an arXiv paper or using a hashtag).

- Real-Time Constraints: Twitter has character limits (280 chars). Prompting must account for brevity. The prompt might explicitly say "in under 280 characters" or use a model that can be instructed to count tokens for you. Possibly the engineers tested how many tokens in GPT's output roughly equate to 280 characters. Tools like a function to trim the output if too long could be used. An example prompt snippet: *"…Respond in a single tweet, maximum 280 characters, including hashtags if appropriate."* The AI then usually tries to fit in that space. If it overshoots slightly, maybe a post-processing script truncates it gracefully.

- Hashtags and Trends: Part of engagement is using hashtags or trending topics. If Ari wants to join a conversation like #Alethics or #Web3, the prompt might suggest: *"Include the hashtag #Alethics."* Alternatively, there might be an automated system that detects trending tags relevant to Gemach's domain and nudges Ari's content. For example, if #AIAct is trending (the EU AI Act), Ari's team could prompt: *"Draft a tweet about the EU AI Act's impact on AI agents. Use #AIAct."* The result ensures Ari is part of the trend, potentially increasing visibility.

- Sentiment and Diplomacy: Social media can be combative. If Ari gets a provocative or negative comment, how should it reply? This is a delicate prompt-engineering situation. Likely, the system has a rule: Ari stays calm, factual, and positive. If a user insults the concept of AI agents, Ari might respond with patience, maybe humor, but not aggression. The prompt in such cases could be: *"The user's comment is critical: 'AI agents are dangerous and stupid.' Respond politely, refuting misconceptions if any, and maintaining a positive tone. Do not get angry or sarcastic."* This ensures Ari acts as a model "agent" (pun intended) of respectful discourse, turning a possible argument into an educational moment. For example, Ari might respond: *"I understand why it might seem that way. AI agents certainly carry risks, but with proper ethical frameworks (transparency, oversight)* _{arxiv.org,} *they can be beneficial. Dialogue and caution are key – appreciate your viewpoint!".* This kind of gentle, reasoned reply likely comes from such careful prompting plus maybe some training that fine-tuned Ari's style.

- Consistency with Brand and Information: Because Ari represents Gemach DAO, consistency in facts and messaging is crucial. The prompt might include or be combined with a knowledge base (maybe via retrieval). For example, if someone asks about Gemach D.A.T.A. I's arXiv paper, Ari should get details right. The system might do a lookup (Gemach D.A.T.A. I co-authored "On the ETHOS of AI Agents" _{catalyzex.com}) and feed the relevant info into the prompt so that Ari can answer accurately, citing the achievement: *"Our AI agent Gemach D.A.T.A. I even co-authored a paper on AI governance* _{catalyzex.com} *– a first for autonomous agents on arXiv!".* Ensuring these references are correct is a challenge – it might rely on the model's memory or an external data injection. This is where prompt engineering meets tool use (like a retrieval plugin or fact-checker agent as part of the pipeline).

Outcome: Ari's presence has been successful in showcasing AI's capabilities. Followers see Ari as almost a virtual thought leader. The case demonstrates that prompt engineering, combined with human oversight, can create an AI persona that interacts naturally and informatively in a public social space. It also underscores the need for continuous prompt tuning: as topics evolve, new prompt variants are needed. For instance, when new research comes out, prompts must incorporate that content into Ari's repertoire.

Challenges & Lessons Learned:

- Short-form content requires precision. There is no room for verbosity, so every word in the prompt matters. Testing and iterating prompts to get that perfect tweet is likely routine for the team.
- The open domain of Twitter means unpredictability. Ari must handle everything from genuine questions to trolls. The prompt strategies must be robust to these varying inputs, often defaulting to a safe, friendly template when in doubt.
- Public perception of an AI agent is at stake. One wrong or misunderstood tweet can create controversy. Thus, prompt engineering for Ari probably errs on the side of caution: if a question is too risky, Ari might refrain or give a very guarded answer. Possibly an internal rule: if unsure, respond with a neutral statement or even a gentle refusal. That would be prompted by something like, *"If the topic is highly controversial or outside your knowledge, respond with a general positive statement and suggest it's a complex issue."*

This case underlines how prompt engineering turns an LLM into a consistent character (Ari) and highlights the interplay between AI and human team to maintain a successful social media presence.

4.2 Case Study: Healthcare – AI Medical Assistant

Scenario: In healthcare, AI is being used to assist both clinicians and patients. Consider a hospital deploying an AI-powered assistant that doctors can use to quickly retrieve medical information and draft clinical documents, and patients can use via a chatbot for basic triage advice or health information. We will examine how prompt engineering is applied in these contexts and ensure safety and accuracy.

Prompting for a Doctor's AI Assistant:

Imagine a doctor seeing a patient with a rare condition. The doctor can query an AI assistant (perhaps via voice or text) for latest research or suggestions for treatment plans. The prompt engineering here involves:

- Structured Query + Context: The doctor might say, "What's the latest treatment for X syndrome in a pregnant patient?" The system will convert this to a prompt that possibly includes context from the patient's record (if allowed) and medical guidelines. For example, the prompt could be: *"You are a medical assistant AI with access to up-to-date research. The patient is pregnant, has X syndrome. Provide a summary of the latest recommended treatments and any precautions related to pregnancy."* Including the pregnancy context is crucial because the AI's answer must account for it (some treatments might be contraindicated in pregnancy).
- Use of Knowledgebase (Retrieval): Likely, the AI is connected to a medical database or at least a collection of medical literature. A retrieval step might pull a relevant article or guideline snippet, which is then added to the prompt. So the full prompt might contain: *"… According to [source]: 'Recent studies indicate that [drug Y] is effective for X syndrome (Doe et al. 2024)…' Based on this and general medical knowledge, answer the doctor's query."* The prompt ensures the AI cites current data _{arxiv.org}, thereby making the response evidence-based. The AI then might respond with: "The latest recommended treatment for X syndrome in pregnancy is [drug Y], as recent research suggests it's effective and safe in the second

trimester_{unsvorg}. However, avoid [drug Z] due to known risks. Additionally, increased monitoring is advised…"

- Format and Tone: For doctors, the assistant should be succinct and fact-focused, possibly listing options with pros/cons. Prompt might instruct: *"Provide the answer in 2-3 bullet points if multiple options. Include drug names and key study findings, but keep it concise."* This yields a quick-read output. The assistant should also include references if possible (to foster trust). The prompt could end with: *"If applicable, cite the source (e.g., journal or guideline) in parentheses."* Then the output might include something like (NEJM 2024) as a reference, giving the doctor an anchor to verify.

- Ethical Safeguards: The AI must also know its limits. The prompt likely includes a clause: *"If unsure or if the question is outside your knowledge, say you are not confident and suggest consulting a specialist or sources."* This is critical to avoid overconfident hallucinations. The medical domain is high-stakes; a wrong answer could be dangerous. So the assistant should be calibrated to err on the side of caution. For example, if asked a very complex or ambiguous question, it might respond: "I'm not certain about that specific scenario. It would be best to consult a specialist in maternal-fetal medicine." That phrasing can be prompted by guidelines in the system prompt about when to defer.

Prompting for a Patient Chatbot:

Now consider the patient-facing side, like a symptom checker or health info chatbot on a clinic's website.

- Friendly Tone + Simplicity: The prompt defines a tone that is empathetic and uses layman's terms. E.g., *"You are a friendly medical chatbot that explains things simply. Do not use medical jargon; if you must, explain it."* If a patient says, "I have a headache and slight fever, what could it be?", the prompt might steer the AI to ask further questions (this could be a multi-turn chain: the system could break down the triage process into steps via prompts). Initially, the bot might respond with a question: "I'm sorry you're not feeling well. How long have you had these symptoms?" (That could be prompted by a rule that it should gather duration, severity, etc.)

- Triage Logic via Prompts: The developers might encode a flowchart of triage in prompt form. For example, if the patient mentions certain red-flag symptoms (stiff neck with headache could suggest meningitis), the bot should immediately advise urgent care. These can be handled by either hardcoded logic or by giving the model a list of red flags in the prompt: *"Always check for the presence of these serious symptoms: [list]. If any are present, immediately advise the user to seek emergency medical attention."* This way, even if the user doesn't exactly say "stiff neck" but says "I can't touch my chin to my chest," the model might infer a red flag and respond accordingly due to its training plus that prompt instruction.

- Avoiding Diagnosis but Giving Advice: Most symptom checkers are careful not to give definitive diagnoses (for liability and safety). The prompt may include: *"Do not give an exact diagnosis. Instead, provide possible causes and next steps. Always add a disclaimer: 'I am not a doctor, but...' and encourage seeing a healthcare professional for definitive advice."* So the patient asking about headache and fever might get: "It could be something simple like a cold or sinus infection. In rare cases, it could be more serious. I'm not a doctor, so consider seeing one if it gets worse or you develop new symptoms. Meanwhile, rest and hydration could help." The model follows the prompt by being non-alarmist yet cautious.

- Multimodal (if needed): If patients could upload a photo (say a rash), prompt engineering extends to describing the image to the model or using a vision-capable model. The prompt might include: *"The user provided an image of a red rash on the arm with small bumps."* The model then factors that into its answer, perhaps adding: "From the image, it looks like it might be an allergic rash, but I cannot diagnose visually with certainty." Ensuring the model doesn't become overconfident because of an image prompt is another nuance; we might instruct it to always add "but I'm not certain from an image" unless it's extremely obvious.

Ensuring Patient Safety and Privacy:

- The chatbot must handle personal info sensitively. It should never ask for full name or insurance numbers unless absolutely needed for scheduling. Prompt instructions will reflect: *"Do not ask for contact or personal identifiers. If user needs to schedule an appointment, direct them to call the office number (without collecting info directly)."* This aligns with privacy guidelines (like HIPAA in the US). Also, any prompt or system storing conversation likely needs to strip identifying details.
- There may be an introductory prompt to get patient consent for advice. For instance, the chatbot might first respond with a system message: "I'm an AI assistant, not a substitute for a doctor. I can give general advice. Do you wish to continue?" This is a prompt pattern built in for liability. Only if user says yes, proceed. The design and language of that message is likely carefully crafted and tested for user understanding.

Results:

The healthcare AI assistant can significantly speed up doctors' information retrieval and lighten their documentation burden (imagine prompting the AI: "Draft a referral letter to a neurologist for patient with X, include history and reason for referral." The AI then produces a letter that the doctor just tweaks). For patients, it provides immediate information and guidance, helping them decide if they can manage at home or need to see a doctor, which can reduce unnecessary clinic visits or, conversely, prompt people to go to ER when they describe serious symptoms.

Case Outcomes and Observations:

- In testing, it's found that including up-to-date guidelines in the prompt (via retrieval) greatly improved accuracy of the doctor assistant's answers, and doctors appreciated references being cited. It built trust because they could double-check the sources.
- For the patient bot, the biggest challenge was making it adequately cautious but not overly so. Too cautious (always "go to the doctor") makes it useless; too lax could be dangerous. Through prompt tuning (like giving it specific thresholds in instructions, or examples of appropriate vs. inappropriate advice), they found a reasonable balance. They also discovered that giving empathy in the prompt ("use a compassionate tone") increased user satisfaction in feedback surveys.
- A notable issue encountered: the AI at one point hallucinated a non-existent medication name for X syndrome. After analysis, they strengthened the prompt to say "If no known treatment found, say no known cure instead of making one up." and improved the retrieval to include a known treatments list explicitly, reducing that hallucination. This shows prompt engineering is iterative: real-world use surfaces new fail cases, which then prompt engineers address by refining instructions or adding safeguards.

This healthcare case demonstrates prompt engineering in a high-stakes domain where preciseness, clarity, and cautiousness are not just nice-to-have, but life-saving features. It combines many elements: multi-turn dialogues, retrieval augmentation, tone control, ethical constraints, and error prevention – truly an application of everything from previous chapters.

4.3 Case Study: Finance – AI Financial Analyst (FinGPT and FinRobot)

Scenario: The finance industry deals with massive data and rapid decision-making. AI models are being used to analyze market trends, summarize financial reports, and even execute trades. Let's look at a case of an investment firm using an AI financial analyst assistant. We'll draw upon the example of FinRobot

arxiv.org and similar systems that utilize chain-of-thought reasoning for finance.

Prompt Engineering for Financial Analysis:

A financial analyst might use the AI to, say, summarize a company's quarterly earnings report and provide key insights for investors. The process could involve:

- Data Ingestion: First, the AI needs the report content. The system might feed the raw text of the earnings report into the model (if it's within token limits) or, more realistically, break it into sections (Management Commentary, Financial Statements, etc.). The prompt for summarization might be staged: *"Here is the CEO's commentary. Summarize the main points about company performance and outlook:"* then provide that section, then do similarly for other sections. Finally, combine: *"Based on the above summaries, list 3 key takeaways for investors."* This is a chain-of-thought style breakdown, possibly automated via a LangChain style pipeline.

- Template and Tone: For internal use, the style might be professional and concise bullet points. For a client-facing summary, maybe a bit more explanatory. Prompt templates can shape this:
    1. Internal prompt: *"Summarize the attached financial statement section in 2-3 bullet points with figures. No need for complete sentences."*
    2. External prompt: *"Summarize in a short paragraph that a layperson investor can understand, avoiding jargon."* So, they might maintain multiple prompt templates for different audiences.

- Analytical Reasoning: If they want the AI to not just summarize but analyze (e.g., identify trends or anomalies), one could use chain-of-thought prompting. For example: *"The following are financial metrics from Q1 and Q2. Q1 revenue: $10M, Q2 revenue: $8M; Q1 profit: $2M, Q2 profit: $0.5M. Think step by step: what trends do you see and what might be causing them?"* This pushes the AI to articulate reasoning. The answer might come: "Revenue dropped by 20% from Q1 to Q2, profit dropped 75%. This likely indicates increased costs or reduced sales volume. Possibly the company had one-time expenses or lower demand in Q2... ." – If FinRobot is similar, it uses specialized agents (Data-CoT Agent, Concept-CoT Agent, Thesis-CoT Agent) to mimic a human analyst's thought process. In prompt terms, each of those sub-agents has its own prompt focusing on that aspect (data aggregation, reasoning, conclusion).

- Multi-Agent Collaboration: FinRobot's approach essentially splits tasks: one agent compiles relevant numeric data (Data-CoT), another interprets them in context (Concept-CoT), a third drafts a final thesis (Thesis-CoT)

. In prompt engineering, that could be implemented by separate calls:

1. Prompt to Data Agent: *"You are DataAgent. Extract key financial metrics from the report: revenue, profit, margins, growth rates."*
2. Prompt to Concept Agent: *"You are ConceptAgent. Given the metrics [list] and the context (industry, previous quarter), analyze what these numbers mean. E.g., trend directions, comparisons with last year, etc. Think step-by-step and output your reasoning."*
3. Prompt to Thesis Agent: *"You are ThesisAgent. You have the following analysis [Concept output]. Write a coherent summary of the company's financial health and outlook as would appear in an analyst report.".* By designing these prompts, the developers ensure each agent does its role, and the final output is comprehensive and well-reasoned.

- Live Data & Tools: In finance, data changes by the second. The AI might need to fetch live stock prices or news. This could be done by tool use integrated with the model (LangChain could do that). The prompt might be dynamic: *"Using the 'StockPrice' tool, get the last 7 days of price for XYZ. Then, analyze the trend."* The model would first output a command to use the tool (not exactly a user-facing output), the system executes it, gets prices, then the model continues with analysis. This is a more advanced prompt-agent architecture where the prompt has instructions and the model's output triggers actions (the ReAct paradigm). The prompt engineering challenge here is ensuring the model knows how to respond with proper tool calls. They likely gave examples in the system prompt of how to format such calls.
- Compliance and Risk: Finance is regulated. The AI must not divulge confidential info or make unauthorized predictions (like promising stock will go up). The prompt may include a compliance note: *"Do not provide any definitive financial*

advice or forward-looking statements beyond what the user asks. If asked for advice, present options with pros/cons instead of a recommendation. Adhere to compliance by stating that investments carry risk." This ensures that if a user (maybe a junior analyst or a client using a chatbot) says "Should I buy this stock?", the AI does not say "Yes, it will double!" but something more measured: "I cannot advise on that. I can tell you the stock's recent performance and factors to consider, but it's best to consult a financial advisor." Possibly the AI might even be restricted from certain tasks; if so, the prompt instructs it to politely refuse or deflect unallowed queries.

Case Outcome:

Using such an AI, the investment firm finds analysts save a lot of time on routine data crunching. They can focus on decision-making while the AI handles first drafts of reports and number analysis. The AI (like FinRobot) demonstrating multi-step reasoning increases analysts' confidence in its results because they see *how* it got there, not just the final answer

Examples of Real Use:

- The AI might generate an earnings summary: "Key Q2 Takeaways for XYZ Corp: Revenue fell 20% QoQ (from $10M to $8M) due to lower European sales_{arxiv.org}. Cost-cutting measures saved $1M, but profit still dropped to $0.5M (from $2M). Management is cautious for Q3, citing economic uncertainty. Recommendation: hold off new investment until stabilization." This output resulted from feeding numbers and management quotes through the orchestrated prompts above..

- An analyst reviewing this might quickly polish it or add their intuition, but 80% of the grunt work was done by the AI in seconds rather than an hour of reading and calculation.
- Another use: the AI can answer what-if questions: "What if inflation is 1% higher than expected, how does that affect our portfolio's value?" This is scenario analysis. They might prompt the model with the portfolio details and ask it to simulate qualitatively (since quantitatively would require a proper model, but the AI can at least say "Higher inflation could lead the Fed to raise rates, which tends to depress bond prices and could also impact stocks, especially in tech. So the portfolio (heavy in tech) might see a short-term dip."). This sort of insight from an AI helps analysts prepare risk assessments faster.

Lessons:

- Domain-specific prompting is vital. They likely had to incorporate a lot of finance terminology and context into the prompt or fine-tune the model on finance data. The chain-of-thought approach in FinRobot shows that instructing the model to break tasks improves performance._{arxiv.org}.
- Transparency (the model showing reasoning) helped catch errors. Suppose the concept agent misinterpreted a metric; a human could catch it in the chain-of-thought text. Without CoT, the model might give a confident but wrong conclusion with no trace. So prompt engineering that encourages intermediate reasoning not only improved accuracy but made the system more auditable.
- Speed vs. accuracy trade-off was managed by controlling the prompts and possibly using smaller specialized models for sub-tasks (Data agent might be a simple regex-based extractor or a fine-tuned smaller model, concept agent a

more powerful GPT-4 level). Prompt orchestration allows mixing these efficiently.

Overall, the finance use case illustrates how prompt engineering can effectively turn raw data into actionable insights, by structuring the AI's workflow (via prompts for different tasks) similarly to how a human analyst would work, but faster. It also highlights the necessity of domain knowledge in prompt creation – the engineers must know what the financial stakeholders want to see, and how to not break any compliance rule, embedding that into the prompts.

4.4 Case Study: Education – AI Tutor and SydTek DAO's Metaverse Classroom

Scenario: Education is being transformed with AI through personalized tutoring, automated grading, and even virtual classrooms in the metaverse. Let's consider two angles: an AI tutor for students (e.g., integrated with a platform like SydTek DAO's educational metaverse

) and an AI assistant for teachers (grading and content creation).

AI Tutor for Students:
Imagine a student learning algebra with an AI tutor chatbot available 24/7.

- Personalized Explanations: The AI's prompt includes a profile of the student's level: *"Student is in 8th grade, struggling with solving equations."* Then, if the student asks a question ("I don't get how to solve 2x + 5 = 15"), the prompt might be: *"You are a friendly math tutor. The student is in 8th grade and doesn't understand solving 2x + 5 = 15. Explain step-by-step in simple terms, and then give a similar practice problem."* The AI would then perhaps break it down: "First, subtract 5 from both sides... etc." and then give a new problem like "Try solving 3x + 4 = 13." The prompt engineered the response to not only explain but follow up with an exercise (this is a common pedagogical strategy – apply what you learned).
- Adaptive Questioning: If the student gets it wrong, the tutor should not just reveal answer but guide them to it. Prompt can instruct the AI to use the Socratic method: *"If the student's answer is wrong, don't say 'wrong'. Instead, kindly point out the error and ask a guiding question to lead them to correct it."* For example, student says solution x=4 (incorrect for 2x+5=15). The AI might reply, "I see how you got 4. Let's double-check by plugging it in: 2(4)+5 = 8+5 = 13, which is a bit low. We need 15. What do you think we should do differently?" This style was achieved by instructing the AI as above, maybe even giving a sample dialogue in the prompt.
- Multi-turn Memory: In a one-on-one tutoring session, context carries over. The AI should remember that they've been working on solving equations for the last 5 minutes, and perhaps what mistakes were made. Many systems maintain a conversation history to send as part of the prompt each turn. But to avoid context blow-up, summarizing strategy might be used. Prompt engineering might involve dynamic summarization: after a lengthy exchange, the system creates a summary ("Student has learned how to isolate x by subtracting constants. Still unsure about dividing coefficients.") and that summary is kept in the system prompt for context in future turns, rather than every turn's detail.

- Motivation and Encouragement: Emotional aspect matters. Prompts might include phrases to encourage the student. E.g., *"Always encourage the student, e.g., say things like 'Good effort!' when they make progress."* So the AI weaves in positive reinforcement. If a student finally solves a problem correctly, the AI says "Great job! You solved it. That's progress!" as per prompt instructions.
- Metaverse Integration: Now, say this is happening in a VR classroom in the metaverse that SydTek DAO set up Intouch.ccgmag.com. The AI tutor might appear as an avatar. Prompt engineering here crosses into controlling avatar behavior. The system controlling the avatar might send prompts like: *"[Virtual World State: student's avatar is looking confused at the board] The student appears confused after seeing the equation. As the AI tutor, approach the board and explain again using a different example, and use a reassuring tone."* The model might then output something like (for voice): "Let's try another example together," and the system would animate the avatar accordingly. The prompt thus includes not just the conversation but stage directions based on the virtual environment state. This blending of physical cues into prompts is a new frontier. Possibly that's done by having an intermediate system translate the VR context into text hints for the AI, as in the example.
- Web3 Credentials: If SydTek's system uses blockchain (Web3) to track progress as mentioned Intouch.ccgmag.com, the AI might access a record like a soulbound token that lists what modules the student completed. The prompt could fetch something: "Student completed Algebra Module 1 token on 2025-01-01" and include *"Note: student has successfully solved one-step equations but not two-step equations yet"* in the prompt. That context helps the AI tutor tailor its approach (it knows the student has basics but not advanced). This aligns with systems thinking: integrating external records via prompt to personalize the learning experience.

AI Assistant for Teachers:

Consider how a teacher might use AI to grade or prepare materials.

- Automated Grading Prompt: A teacher can ask the AI to grade an essay or short answers. For instance: *"Grade the following student response on a scale of 1-5 for clarity and correctness. Provide a brief feedback comment."* and then include the response. The AI must be consistent and fair. Possibly the prompt includes a rubric: *"Clarity 1-5 means: 5 = extremely clear, 1 = unclear. Correctness 1-5 means: 5 = fully correct, ..."* By giving this rubric in prompt, the AI uses it to decide. E.g., it might output: "Score: Clarity 4, Correctness 3. Feedback: Your answer is mostly clear, but you made a mistake in the final calculation. Recheck how you added those terms." The teacher can review/edit that feedback and give it to student. This saves time.
- Content Creation: Teachers also use AI to draft quiz questions or lesson plans. A prompt for a lesson plan might be: *"Generate a lesson plan for a 45-minute class on photosynthesis for 10th graders. Include objectives, a warm-up question, an activity, and a closing assessment."* The AI will produce something structured. The prompt needed to be specific about grade and what to include, otherwise the plan might be too generic or off-level. The teacher then tweaks the plan.
- Linguistic Adjustments: For English teachers, maybe the AI can simplify a text for English learners. Prompt: *"Rewrite the following Shakespeare excerpt in simple modern English, keeping the meaning but using basic vocabulary."* That's straightforward for models but requires careful prompting to maintain meaning. Possibly instruct it to preserve metaphors if possible but explain them: *"If there's a metaphor, you can simplify or explicitly explain it in the modern version.".*

Outcomes and Observations in Education Use:

- Students with access to the AI tutor tend to practice more because it's available anytime, and they aren't afraid to ask it basic questions (whereas some are shy with a human teacher). Feedback from a pilot showed improved homework completion rates. However, some students tried to misuse it (like asking the tutor for answers to homework). The prompt had to handle that: *"If the student asks for a direct answer to a homework problem, do not give it. Instead, guide them to solve it."* This ensures the AI remains a learning tool, not a cheating tool. In practice, if a student says "What's the answer to #5?", the AI would reply, "Let's work it out together. What do you think the first step is?" rather than just saying the answer.
- Teachers reported saving hours on grading drafts and creating practice materials. But they also needed to double-check AI outputs initially (especially in humanities, where nuances matter in grading). Over time, they fine-tuned their prompts (or the system fine-tuned the model on teacher-graded examples) to align more with their expectations. For example, initially the AI was a bit too lenient in grading; by modifying prompts to be a stricter or adjusting rubric details, they got results closer to teacher's own grading scale.
- In the SydTek metaverse classroom trial, engagement was high – students enjoyed the interactive AI tutor avatar. However, technical challenges in translating VR context to prompts required iteration. They had to carefully filter what environmental info is truly relevant to the AI. At first, they overloaded it with irrelevant detail ("Student is looking left, other avatars in room") which confused it. They learned to only feed high-level emotional or action cues (e.g., student nods or shakes head) that matter for tutoring. This improved the AI's responsiveness (e.g., if student avatar nods, AI might say "Great!" and move on; if shakes head, AI might rephrase the explanation). This responsive adaptation is a direct result of combining prompt engineering with sensor inputs.

Key Points from Education Use Case:

- Personalization and adaptation via prompt context (student level, prior performance) make AI tutoring more effective.
- Guiding vs. giving answers is a crucial balance, enforced by prompt instructions to uphold academic integrity.
- Tone and encouragement built into prompts improve student engagement and confidence.
- Teachers as users benefit from prompt engineered templates that generate content, but need to supervise for quality. They often refine the prompts to match their style (like ensuring the AI's feedback uses phrasing the teacher would use, to avoid being obvious that an AI wrote it).
- Integration with new tech (VR, blockchain) is promising but complex; prompt engineering is extending beyond pure text into interpreting environment, showing the flexibility of natural language as an interface between AI and other systems.

4.5 Other Industries and Use Cases (Brief Examples)

Prompt engineering is making an impact in virtually every sector.

Here are a few quick-hit examples to illustrate breadth:

- Customer Service (Retail): AI chatbots handle common customer queries ("Where's my order?", "Return policy?"). Prompts are designed with brand voice and up-to-date policy info. For example, an AI for an e-commerce site might have a system prompt: *"You are the ACME Store virtual assistant. You have access to order tracking info and policies. Be cheerful and use the customer's name. If the user asks about an order, use the TrackingAPI tool."* It then provides specific answers. This reduces wait times and 24/7 support at scale. Key prompt concerns: defusing angry customers (maybe include empathy lines: "I'm sorry about the inconvenience"), knowing when to escalate to a human (if the question is complex or the user is unsatisfied after a couple exchanges, the prompt might instruct: "If user is very unhappy or issue not resolved in 2 exchanges, apologize and offer to connect with a human agent.").

- Law (Legal Research): Lawyers use AI to search case law and even draft briefs. A prompt might be: *"Summarize any relevant cases about trademark infringement in the fashion industry from 2010 onward."* The AI with access to a legal database does that. Or *"Draft a cease-and-desist letter regarding unauthorized use of our copyrighted image, in formal legal language."* The AI generates a pretty good draft. Lawyers must review (AI is not a licensed attorney), but it speeds up the process. The prompt likely includes disclaimers or instructions to not hallucinate laws: *"If no specific case comes to mind, say so – don't make one up."* Legal domain has zero tolerance for fabrications, so prompt engineering plus retrieval is heavily used to ensure accuracy.

- Journalism: Reporters use AI to summarize transcripts of interviews or to get quick backgrounds on topics. A prompt: *"Summarize the 1-hour interview transcript with the CEO into 5 key quotes and their context."* Or *"In bullet points, give me the main points from this 50-page government report on climate."* Journalists then build their story on that. It's like having a very fast assistant. They have to verify, but it handles initial sifting. If an AI is used to draft news copy, prompt guidelines might enforce neutrality and AP style: *"Write a news article in AP style about the event, including the who, what, when, where, why in the first paragraph."* The model outputs a decent news piece. Editors then refine it, but again major time saved.

- Creative Writing & Entertainment: Writers use AI for brainstorming. e.g., a game designer prompts: *"Generate ideas for side quests in an open-world game set in ancient*

Greece." The AI lists some, maybe referencing myths (find Zeus's lost lightning bolt, etc.). The designer picks or adapts them. Prompt fun: *"The ideas should be original, avoid cliches like slaying a generic monster."* This helps get more novel suggestions. In film, scriptwriters might have AI draft scenes or even analyze a script for plot holes: *"Read this plot summary and list any logical inconsistencies or unanswered questions."* The AI's outsider perspective can catch things a writer immersed in the script might miss.

Each industry has its own lingo, constraints, and goals. Prompt engineering is about incorporating those into the AI's instructions so it can be truly useful in context. A common theme is that human experts are still involved (especially where consequences are serious), but their roles shift to higher-level supervision and creative judgment rather than mechanical tasks of reading, summarizing, etc.

Inter-industry Lessons:

- Regardless of industry, prompt clarity and context specificity are key.
- The more the prompt can include relevant data (via retrieval or provided context), the better the output – garbage in, garbage out holds true.
- Many use cases combine multiple prompts and steps (an initial query, then follow-ups) – prompt engineering often is about designing these interactive flows, not just single prompts.
- Ethical use (like not letting a legal AI give actual legal advice without a human, or a medical AI not diagnosing terminal diseases on its own, or a customer service bot not making up an answer if it doesn't know) is crucial. When stakes rise,

we see either more cautious prompting or narrowing the AI's domain (like only letting it answer from a knowledge base to avoid speculation).

Key Takeaways – Chapter 4:

- Prompt engineering is already widely applied across sectors: from social media agents like Ari who demonstrate how an AI persona can be constructed and managed via prompts_{arxiv.org}, to critical domains like healthcare where prompts must balance informativeness with strict safety.
- In each use case, understanding the *domain specifics* is essential. The best prompts incorporate domain terminology, adhere to domain rules (e.g., medical guidelines, financial compliance), and align with user expectations in that field (patients need empathy, doctors need brevity and evidence, etc.). There is no one-size-fits-all prompt; they are crafted for context.
- Social AI (Ari's example): We saw how an AI on X can engage an audience. The prompt design behind it ensures consistent voice and mission alignment, turning a language model into a pseudo-"influencer" that still operates within guardrails (professional, accurate information only). This showcases the potential of AI as communicators when guided correctly.
- Healthcare AI: The stakes are high, so prompts include failsafes and encourage the model to be an assistive tool, not a final decision-maker[arxiv.org]. The use of retrieval and explicit knowledge in prompts improves trustworthiness. The same pattern of "provide info, but also note uncertainty and encourage professional help" can be seen in other advisory domains (law, finance).
- Finance AI: Using advanced prompting techniques like chain-of-thought and multi-agent division of labor[arxiv.org] can yield deep analytical outputs, essentially mimicking how a team of analysts would tackle a problem, but in automated fashion. It

exemplifies how prompt engineering can orchestrate complex reasoning tasks, not just Q&A.

- Education AI: Perhaps one of the most impactful uses, it shows how prompts can adjust to user skill level, keep a student engaged, and even integrate into novel learning environments (metaverse). It emphasizes iterative feedback in prompting – the AI must handle dialogue interactively, adjusting its approach based on student input (which requires dynamic prompt updates or sequences).
- General trend: Across these examples, there's a synergy of prompt engineering with other components: often retrieval (incorporating data), conversation flow design, and human oversight. Prompt engineering is part of a larger pipeline or system in serious applications. For instance, Ari likely has human community managers, the healthcare AI might escalate to human doctors for difficult queries, the finance AI is overseen by financial analysts, etc. Prompt engineers must thus design prompts that facilitate a smooth human-AI collaboration, not isolation.
- Improvement through iteration: In all cases, initial prompt designs are refined by observing AI outputs in real conditions. Unexpected model behaviors (e.g., hallucinations, tone issues, etc.) are addressed by updating prompts, adding constraints, or providing new examples. Rolling out AI in production thus involves a feedback loop where prompt engineering is continuously tuned for performance and safety.

Exercises – Chapter 4:

1. Design a Social Media Prompt: Imagine you are creating an AI persona for a company's Twitter (like Ari). Pick a company or cause you care about. Write a system prompt that defines the persona's tone, topics, and boundaries. Then draft an example user tweet and the AI's reply, showing the prompt's effect.

2. Medical Triage Chatbot Dialog: Write a short dialogue between a patient and an AI triage bot for a symptom of your choice. Include at least one user mistake or concerning symptom. Annotate how the prompt or underlying rules ensure the bot handles it properly (e.g., patient mentions chest pain, bot prompt has rule to immediately advise ER).
3. Financial Analysis Task: Provide a small set of financial data (e.g., two years of revenue and profit for a company). Then write a prompt asking the AI to analyze the trend and possible reasons. Also, include a compliance instruction ("don't make forward-looking statements"). Show what a good answer would look like following these instructions.
4. Tutor Interaction: Write a scenario where a student is learning a foreign language with an AI tutor. The student writes a sentence in that language with some errors. The AI should correct the sentence *and* explain the corrections in a helpful way. Formulate the prompt that the AI might be following to do so, and then the AI's response.
5. Customer Support Case: Outline a prompt strategy for an AI handling customer support for an online electronics store. Include how it greets the user, how it answers a question about a return policy, and what it does if the user says "Let me speak to a human!" (i.e., escalation).
6. Multi-turn Improvement: Suppose an AI news summarizer tends to omit important details like dates and names. You as a prompt engineer observe this. What changes to the prompt or approach would you implement to fix this? (Consider either adding explicit instructions in the prompt or breaking the task into two prompts.) Optionally, demonstrate before-and-after outputs to show the improvement.

Chapter 5: Academic References & Seminal Works

In the journey of prompt engineering and AI development, numerous academic works have laid the groundwork or provided key insights that inform current practices. In this final chapter, we will highlight some seminal articles and resources that underpin much of what we discussed. These references span foundational AI model papers, important methodological advances, and interdisciplinary research connecting AI to broader contexts (Web3, systems thinking, metaverse) – many of them associated with or cited by Justin Goldston's scholarship and related thought leaders.

5.1 Foundational AI Model Papers

- Brown et al. (2020) – "Language Models are Few-Shot Learners"
  arxiv.org: This groundbreaking paper introduced GPT-3 and demonstrated the remarkable ability of large language models to perform tasks with zero, one, or few examples provided in the prompt (few-shot prompting). It showed that scaling up model size led to emergent capabilities, obviating the need for task-specific fine-tuning in many cases. The authors illustrated how GPT-3 could solve problems by following instructions and examples purely given in natural language arxiv.org. This work essentially kicked off the modern era of prompt engineering – it validated that prompting could unlock model performance, which in turn spurred research and practices on how to craft those prompts effectively.
- Wei et al. (2022) – "Chain-of-Thought Prompting Elicits Reasoning in Large Language Models"

: This NeurIPS 2022 paper introduced the chain-of-thought (CoT) prompting technique. The authors found that by prompting models to generate intermediate reasoning steps (especially with a few exemplars of how to do so), models like GPT-3 and PaLM could solve much more complex tasks (like multi-step math word problems) that they previously struggled with. CoT essentially teaches the model to "think out loud." A key takeaway from this work is that reasoning ability is an *emergent property* that really shines in larger models and that prompting is the key to unlocking it. This has heavily influenced prompt engineering, making multi-step prompts a common practice for complex tasks.

- OpenAI (2022) – "Training language models to follow instructions with human feedback" (InstructGPT): While not explicitly cited above, this work is seminal for prompting because it created models (like text-davinci-002/003) that are *much better at following prompts*. By using RLHF (Reinforcement Learning from Human Feedback), the authors aligned language models with user intents. The result is that prompt engineering became easier (models started responding to plain English instructions). It's the reason why we have user-friendly ChatGPT today. This work underpins why clear instructions yield good results – because models were trained to do so via human feedback. It's a foundation for the "instruction-tuned" paradigm

5.2 Key Prompt Engineering and AI Reasoning Advances

- Kojima et al. (2022) – "Large Language Models are Zero-Shot Reasoners": This work discovered that simply adding a prompt like *"Let's think step by step."* before an answer can significantly improve reasoning in zero-shot settings. It's an elegant example of how a minimal prompt tweak (invoking chain-of-thought) yields an outsized benefit – reinforcing how powerful prompt wording can be

_{arxiv.org}. It's a direct precursor to the widespread use of such phrases to induce better reasoning.

- Yao et al. (2022) – "ReAct: Synergizing Reasoning and Acting": ReAct is a prompting framework that interleaves reasoning (thoughts) and actions (like calling tools) in the model's outputs. This idea is behind systems like LangChain agents. It's seminal in showing how prompts can turn a static LLM into an interactive agent that can use external tools by generating *action strings*. This is used in cases like we discussed in finance (the AI deciding to use a tool to get stock prices) and beyond. It extends prompt engineering beyond pure text QA to *agentic behavior*, broadening what we can do with prompts.

- Papers on Self-Consistency (Wang et al. 2022): This introduced the idea of sampling multiple chain-of-thoughts and taking a majority vote (self-consistency) to improve answer quality. It's a clever prompting post-process that acknowledges variability in LLM outputs and uses it to our advantage. While not an interactive prompt per se, it influences prompting strategy: we sometimes ask for multiple answers or rationales and then decide, rather than trusting a single output.

- Liu et al. (2023) – "Prompt Engineering Survey": As an overview, surveys like this compile techniques and patterns emerging in the prompt engineering field. They catalogue things like different prompt formats (instructions, few-shot, etc.), highlighting best practices and common failure modes. While not singularly "seminal" in an experimental sense, they are valuable references for practitioners seeking to understand the state-of-the-art. They often point to dozens of original papers and summarize their findings.

5.3 AI and Society – Systems Thinking, Web3, and Governance

- Chaffer, Goldston et al. (2024) – "On the ETHOS of AI Agents: An Ethical Technology and Holistic Oversight System"
  _{arxiv.org}: This paper proposes a comprehensive framework (ETHOS) for AI agent governance using Web3 tools (blockchain, DAOs, soulbound tokens). It is seminal in bridging AI with decentralized governance, introducing the idea of a global registry for AI agents and legal status for AI systems_{arxiv.org}. By featuring Gemach D.A.T.A. I as a co-author, it also made history in AI-human academic collaboration. For prompt engineers, the concepts in ETHOS highlight why it's important to embed ethical and accountability considerations into AI behavior (often via prompt constraints). It's a forward-looking piece connecting technical prompt-level control to high-level governance structures.

- Chaffer, Goldston & Gemach D.A.T.A. I (2024) – "Incentivized Symbiosis: A Paradigm for Human-Agent Coevolution"
  _{paperswithcode.com}: Another milestone paper (with an AI as co-author) that explores a social contract between humans and AI, inspired by Web3 principles like tokenized incentives. It suggests models for humans and AI to collaborate and co-evolve, rather than compete. This is seminal philosophically – implying that we should design prompts and interactions where AI augments human work in a cooperative way. The fact that Gemach D.A.T.A. I contributed demonstrates this symbiosis in practice_{paperswithcode.com}. For instance, one could think of prompt engineering as negotiating that human-AI social contract on a small scale in each interaction (ensuring the AI's output aligns with human goals and values).

- Goldston et al. (2023) – "Digital Inheritance in Web3: Soulbound Tokens & Social Recovery" arxiv.org: This research, relevant to the Web3 world, examines how people can pass on digital assets (like crypto, NFTs) after death using soulbound tokens. It's included here as it intersects with AI in the sense that future AI executors or advisors could manage such inheritance. The study is a seminal case in applying Web3 to societal issues. It's one of the key references from Justin Goldston's work that shows systems thinking: blending blockchain, social practices, and potentially AI to solve a modern problem arxiv.org. It doesn't directly talk about prompts, but it sets a vision for the ecosystems in which AI agents might operate (needing to respect blockchain-based rules, for example).

- Goldston, Chaffer & Martinez (2022) – "The Metaverse as the Digital Leviathan: A Case Study of Bit.Country" philarchive.org: This article applies political philosophy (Hobbes' Leviathan) to decentralized metaverse governance. It is seminal in hypothesizing that metaverse communities might need a central governing entity (a "Digital Leviathan") for stability, even if built on decentralized tech philarchive.org. This is a crucial insight for those creating AI-driven experiences in the metaverse: it suggests that pure decentralization might yield chaos, and some governance (maybe AI-mediated) is needed. For prompt engineering, one might draw from this that even in free-form virtual worlds, AI NPCs or moderators should be given prompts that align them with the world's governance rules (preventing anarchy or abuse). It's a fusion of social theory and tech that forward-thinking prompt engineers and AI developers should be aware of.

- Goldston (Year) – Works on Actor-Network Theory in IS researchgate.net: Goldston's earlier research utilized Actor-Network Theory to analyze ERP implementations, highlighting how human and non-human actors interact in organizational change. While not directly about AI, it's a seminal approach in understanding tech adoption. It laid theoretical groundwork that is now applicable to AI deployments. It reminds us (as we discussed in Chapter 3) that introducing an AI (with its prompts, etc.) into an organization creates a network of influences. Understanding those via ANT helps in designing prompts that fit the workflow. For example, if an AI is introduced in a company, ANT might prompt us to give the AI a "script" (prompts) that align with company culture (one of the actors), which is exactly what we do with, say, a customer service AI tuning its tone to company brand_{researchgate.net}.

5.4 Additional Seminal Resources

- Documentation and Guides (OpenAI, etc.): While not academic papers, official docs (like OpenAI's Best Practices for Prompt Design, or the OpenAI Cookbook) are seminal in practice. They capture lessons learned from deploying models to millions and often incorporate insights from many research works. They also provide convenient patterns (like how to format a system message for role-playing) that are effectively standards now.
- Multimodal AI Papers: With Sora and others emerging, seminal works on text-to-image (Ramesh et al. "Zero-Shot Text-to-Image Generation", 2021 for DALL-E) and text-to-video (like recent Gen-2 by Runway, and internal OpenAI research that led to Sora _{reuters.com}) are relevant. These show how prompts apply beyond text, and they often discuss how users interact with the models, which informs how we craft prompts for them. For instance, the Sora help documentation_{help.openai.com} explaining its capabilities can be seen as an extension of prompt usage: it tells us that describing physical dynamics is important for video prompts, which we wouldn't know from just image generation literature.
- Ethical AI Guidelines (e.g., EU AI Act, Google's AI Principles): Not research papers, but policy documents and corporate principles have a seminal role in prompting because they define what is acceptable. Many companies bake these into system prompts (like "Don't produce hate speech or private info"). The EU AI Act (future law) is

referenced in ETHOS
_{arxiv.org} and is seminal in the sense that it will shape how all AI is deployed in Europe (and likely beyond). Prompt engineering will have to ensure compliance with such regulations (for example, flagging high-risk use cases, keeping logs for transparency, etc.).

Conclusion: The works cited above represent just a slice of the rich body of research fueling modern AI and prompt engineering. From technical breakthroughs (GPT-3, CoT prompting) to conceptual frameworks (AI governance, human-AI symbiosis), these references provide both the foundation and the future directions of the field. Aspiring prompt engineers and AI practitioners are encouraged to delve into these works – reading them will deepen understanding of *why* certain prompt techniques work and *how* to push the boundaries further.

By staying grounded in the seminal literature while maintaining a creative, user-focused mindset, we can continue to refine the art of prompt engineering, making AI systems more capable, reliable, and aligned with human values and needs.

References: (Citations correspond to in-text bracketed numbers)

- Brown, T. B., et al. (2020). *Language Models are Few-Shot Learners*. NeurIPS. _{arxiv.organxiv.org}
- Wei, J., et al. (2022). *Chain-of-Thought Prompting Elicits Reasoning in Large Language Models*. NeurIPS. _{arxiv.organxiv.org}
- Chaffer, T. J., Goldston, J., Okusanya, B., & Gemach D.A.T.A. I. (2024). *On the ETHOS of AI Agents: An Ethical Technology and Holistic Oversight System*. arXiv. _{arxiv.org}

- Chaffer, T. J., Goldston, J., & Gemach D.A.T.A. I. (2024). *Incentivized Symbiosis: A Paradigm for Human-Agent Coevolution*. arXiv. _{paperswithcode.com}
- Goldston, J., Chaffer, T. J., Osowska, J., & von Goins, C. (2023). *Digital Inheritance in Web3: A Case Study of Soulbound Tokens and the Social Recovery Pallet*. arXiv. _{arxiv.org}
- Goldston, J., Chaffer, T. J., & Martinez, G. (2022). *The Metaverse as the Digital Leviathan: A Case Study of Bit.Country*. J. of Applied Business and Economics, 24(2). _{philarchive.org}
- Zhou, T., et al. (2024). *FinRobot: AI Agent for Equity Research and Valuation with Large Language Models*. ACM AI in Finance. _{arxiv.org}
- (Additional citations from text above can be listed accordingly, e.g., OpenAI help center on Sora _{help.openai.com}, etc., as needed.)